CONCEPT
CARS

Martin Derrick

Happy Fathers Day

Love,

Mike and Ann

CONCEPT CARS

Martin Derrick

Published by TAJ Books 2005

27, Ferndown Gardens,
Cobham,
Surrey,
UK,
KT11 2BH

All notations of errors or omissions (author inquiries, permissions) concerning the content of this book should be addressed to TAJ Books 27, Ferndown Gardens, Cobham, Surrey, UK, KT11 2BH, info@tajbooks.com.

Paperback ISBN 1-84406-055-1
Hardback ISBN 1-84406-066-7

Printed in China.
1 2 3 4 5 10 09 08 07 06 05

CONTENTS

INTRODUCTION

Above: *1954 Motorama*

At the outset of the automobile industry, every car that was built was a concept car, in the sense that each was individually manufactured and individually designed and was an experiment in technology and design. So back in 1789 when Nicholas Cugnot built what is generally reckoned to be the world's first self-propelling vehicle, his vastly heavy three-wheeled steam-driven carriage (which reached the heady speed of 5 km/h (3 mph) then failed to take its first corner and crashed) was an exercise that pushed the boundaries of engineering.

Those boundaries were pushed still further with the development of the internal combustion engine and the creation in 1885 of Karl Benz's first tricycle car. After that, the automobile industry witnesses a technological and stylistic free for all as Panhard in France, the Duryea brothers in the USA, Henry Ford, Ransom Olds and many others around the industrialised world developed faster, more practical, more efficient and more reliable cars. But what all these early efforts had in common was that they were breaking new ground at every stage.

Now, even though in the 21st century the automobile industry is fully mature, there is always room for the most imaginative, brave and creative minds in the business to come up with new ideas and new concepts.

In addition, perhaps the biggest draws at each of the world's major motor shows are the concept cars on display. Some are mad, some are bad. Some are thought-provoking and some are superficial. Some show glimpses of genuinely new

technologies, or packaging, or design. Some are just playful flights of fancy. But they provide the glitz and the glamour that every motor show needs. And they provide a brief look into what the future might just hold for us all.

So concept cars play a vital role in the automotive industry. They offer an opportunity for manufacturers and design houses to test new ideas and investigate new designs. Once most concept cars were simply explorations of style but the very best combine form with function because good design doesn't just look good, it also has to perform well. So good design might mean better functionality, better comfort, better safety, better fuel consumption. It could also mean more driving pleasure, more practicality and more environmental friendliness.

In the early days of motoring, some extraordinary concepts were proposed. In

1921, for example, Marcel Leyat devised his Leyat Helica, a propeller-driven car. Hopelessly impractical, the driver had to steer the machine while looking through the propeller and his life was made even less straightforward by the fact that Leyat chose to make his car rear-wheel steered.

Just eight years later, in 1929, Opel produced a far more practical but still scary device, the Opel RAK 2 rocket car. Powered by 12 rocket motors it achieved a top speed of 230 km/h (143 mph) at the Avus test track in Germany, but thankfully it was not further developed for road use.

Despite these earlier diversions, the concept car as we know it today was probably first created in 1938 by General Motor's chief designer Harley J. Earl. He built the famous 'Y-Job' that year in co-operation with GM's Buick Division, and this became the first of a string of GM concepts over the following years.

Earl did not use the term 'concept car', preferring to describe the Y-Job as a 'dream car'. He said at the time that it gave the stylist a tool for advanced research comparable to the laboratory and proving ground used by the scientist and engineer and added, "The dream car has become a world famous symbol of the American public's ever-growing fascination with the life it can expect in the future".

According to Earl, the dream car stimulates the stylist to creative thinking because it allows him to build in three dimensions the futuristic ideas he conceives which are too advanced to be applied to the design of next year's model: "This catches and brings to life for the motorist many design ideas which might otherwise be lost".

But there is more to a dream car that this, said Earl: "Once built and exhibited the dream car provides factual public reaction to its new features through customer research. Proof of advance acceptability encourages a manufacturer to spend the money to put an idea into production far sooner than he would if he had doubts about its acceptance".

The Y-Job itself was a ground-breaking piece of design (see pages 74-75) that exhibited a number of firsts including the world's first electrically operated convertible top, first power windows and first extension of the fenders into the front doors.

This was followed by two further important GM dream cars, the LeSabre

of 1951 and the XP-300, also of 1951. The LeSabre featured the first panoramic windscreen which later became standard throughout the automobile industry.

The Buick XP-300 embodied many of the industry's most advanced ideas including a new supercharged 355-horsepower engine.

But GM did more than effectively invent the concept car. It also created a whole new way of bringing these dream cars – and of course its production cars, which since the end of the Second World War were now starting to become available again – to the eyes of the public.

It staged a series of eight GM Motoramas from 1949 to 1961, in essence private General Motors Motor Shows that moved around the country to different venues.

Below: *1961 Ford Gyron Show Car*

The first of these took place in 1949 in two cities, New York and Boston when 591,971 people flocked through the doors. The following year a further 320,000 visited the 1950 Motorama which was held in New York only.

January 1953 at the Waldorf Astoria hotel in New York City, saw yet another Motorama development: it was the first of these events to feature futuristic dream cars. Over 300,000 visited, mostly to see the star of the show, Chevrolet's first ever Corvette. The show stopper, and most famous dream car, was the Corvette.

GM used the Motoramas to gauge the public's reactions to the different dream cars and mechanical and technological innovations. The fact is that these dream cars influenced the design of General Motors cars for years to come and the Motoramas were becoming so successful that each year, GM strove to make the

events more elaborate than ever before.

So, for example, at the 1954 Motorama, also held at the Waldorf Astoria in New York, a 27-piece orchestra complete with a 12-voice chorus provided a musical background for six shows each day. The real star of the show was the experimental gas turbine XP 21 Firebird which was displayed on an elevated turntable alongside six other dream cars.

The 1954 Motorama was bigger still, and it was the subject of a Bob Hope-hosted special CBS TV preview which brought the show to millions of American viewers. On a huge stage in the Waldorf Astoria, all of GM's production cars were on show, suspended on steel arms that left the cars hovering above a lake of water.

Strategically displayed around the huge ballroom were the "dream cars" selected for the show.

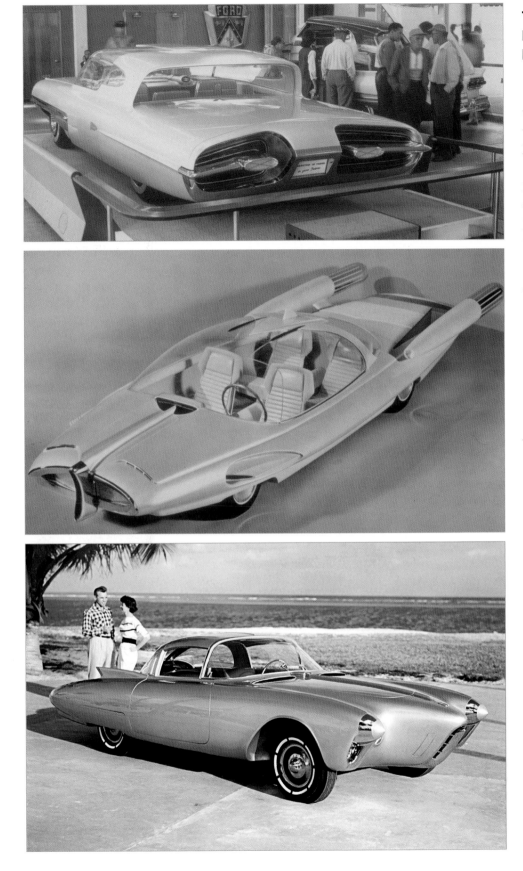

Top: *1958 Ford La Galaxie*
Middle: *1958 Ford X-2000*
Bottom: *Oldsmobile Golden Rocket*

The 1956 Motorama featured the Firebird II, the second of three turbine cars that would appear in the Motoramas. Five new Dream Cars for 1956 were on display in addition to the Firebird II: Chevrolet's Impala, Pontiac's Club de Mer, Oldsmobile's Golden Rocket, Buick's Centurion and Cadillac's Brougham Town Car.

The 1959 and 1961 Motoramas used production cars and elaborate displays as the show's main draws and in fact the 1959 show displayed only one dream car, the Firebird III gas turbine car.

But GM was not alone in using concept cars as a means of attracting the public's attention. In 1950, for example, the British Rover Company produced its Jet 1 concept, the first car in the world to be powered by a gas turbine engine. The mid-engined two-seater roadster reached 244 km/h (152 mph).

If the Rover Jet 1 showcased new engine technology, the Alfa Romeo Disco Volante of 1952 highlighted sheer design. Its name means 'Flying Saucer', which reflects its ovoid proportions, but it was also undoubtedly aerodynamic because despite a relatively small 2.0-litre engine, it still managed a top speed of 219 km/h (136 mph).

The same year Ford showed its X-100 cabriolet which anticipated the styling of future models, including the Thunderbird. Also in that vintage year for concepts came the Pinin Farina-designed Lancia PF 200 Spider with its circular jet-engine grille and the Bertone-styled Fiat-Abarth 1600 which again relied on aeronautical motifs in its appearance.

1953 was the year of the first of the BAT cars. Nothing to do with Batman, but a series of three BAT (Berlinetta Aerodinamica Tecnica) cars produced by Bertone to investigate advanced styling borrowed from the world of aviation.

The first of these, confusingly called BAT 5, was based on Alfa Romeo mechanicals and had a futuristic style by Franco Scaglione. The second, called BAT 7, was unveiled in 1954 at the Turin Motor Show and was again designed by Scaglione. It had even longer rear wings which turned in on the car's tail spine. All its styling derived from aviation, from the extraordinary fins, to the air intakes made to look like jet engine intakes. The third, BAT 9, was produced in 1955, again based on Alfa mechanicals but this time with slightly more restrained styling.

Around the same time GM came up with the first Firebird, another futuristic concept powered by a gas turbine engine and deliberately styled to look like a space rocket. When it was revealed at the 1954 Paris Motor Show it became the immediate star of the show.

If these concepts looked futuristic, Ford's 1958 LaGalaxie looked like nothing on earth. It's unlikely that any concept has even been produced that was quite as ugly and ill-proportioned. This attempt at science fiction had no steering wheel, a radar system to warn of other vehicles and even a rudimentary information screen.

The late 1950's obsession with aeronautical imagery just wouldn't go away and Cadillac was next onto the bandwagon with its Cyclone concept in 1959. It had a glass canopy that hinged upwards to allow access via sliding doors and massive rear fins, but it also at least had a sensible powertrain – a 6.4-litre V8 producing 350 bhp.

Ford's Gyron of 1961 was a considerably less practical proposition mainly because it only had two wheels and it was allegedly kept upright by a gyroscopic stabiliser. Driver and passenger sat in tandem while electronics controlled navigation and cruise control.

Again from Ford, the Seattle of 1962 was a mock-up even less likely to make it anywhere near production, mainly because it was proposed to have interchangeable power units, either electric or nuclear. The only interesting aspect was its four smaller front wheels, something that would turn up in Formula 1 many years later on the Tyrell P34.

By the mid-1960's the aeronautical conceits were finally consigned to history and designers cold concentrate on more realistic designs. One of the most successful of all was the Alfa Romeo Canguro which was penned by Giorgetto

Below: *Bertone Alfa Romeo Carabo*
Bottom: *Bertone Alfa Romeo Canguro*

Above: *VW-Porsche Tapiro*

Giugiaro for Bertone before the famous designer left to set up his own ItalDesign business. Based around the Alfa Tubulare chassis, and with the 1.6-litre in-line four-cylinder engine from the Alfa Giula SS, the Canguro was unveiled at the Paris Motor Show in 1964. It has magnificent proportions, elegant lines and fabulous presence. The Canguro proved Giugiaro, even at an early age, was one of the very top designers.

This was undoubtedly the golden age of the Italian design houses. Pininfarina came up with two stunning Ferrari concepts in 1968 and 1969, the 512 Berlinetta Speciale and the 250 PS. At the same time ItalDesign produced the stunning wedge-shaped Bazzarrini Manta, Ghia penned another wedge design, the Serenissima, and Bertone produced the gullwinged Alfa Romeo Carabo.

Then in 1970, they all went one better. Piinfarina produced the extraordinary Ferrari Modulo, whose canopy slid rearwards to allow access to the interior.

Based around a Ferrari 512S chassis, it was first revealed as a black car at the Geneva Show and was then repainted white and shown at venues all round the world.

The same year ItalDesign produced the VW-Porsche Tapiro, Ghia produced the de Tomaso Vignale and Bertone produced its Lancia Stratos. All were wedge-shaped mid-engined GTs that captured the futuristic mood of the times. Sharp edges remained the name of the game in the coming years, characterised by concepts such as the Lamborghini Bravo that was designed at Bertone by Marcello Gandini, the man who would later create other Lamborghini masterpieces. ItalDesign's Maserati Coupé and Maserati Medici were both 2+2 concepts that looked as if they were production-ready, though Michelotti's Lancia Mizar, also produced in 1974,

Right: *Opel Experimental GT*
Below: *Italdesign Taxi*

Above: *Oldsmobile Aerotech*

never came close to manufacture because of its highly-complicated gullwing doors and pop-up headlights.

One of the most influential designs of the later 1970's was ItalDesign's Lancia Megagamma, probably the world's first true MPV.

ItalDesign's obsession at that time with maximising interior space also lead to the creation of the Taxi which again influenced many later designs.

Showing how a concept can be used both to gauge public reaction but also to prepare the public for a radical change in design direction, the Ford Probe III of 1981 clearly showed the rounded style of the forthcoming Ford Sierra production model. The Probe IV, revealed at the 1983 Detroit Show was a study in advanced aerodynamics and achieved a record 0.15 Cd.

As the 1980's progressed, so the Japanese motor manufacturers started showing bolder and brasher concepts, particularly at the Tokyo Motor Show which gained the reputation for being the venue for some of the most radical concepts and prototypes.

Nissan revealed the Cue-X in 1985 and in the same year Mitsubishi produced the MP90X and Mazda the MX-03.

The following year GM came back to the fore with the Oldsmobile Aerotech, a GT designed specifically for breaking speed records. With up to 1000 bhp on tap from a four-cylinder turbocharged 2.0-litre engine, it achieved 430 km/h (267 mph) at the Fort Stockton, Texas racetrack driven by legendary racer A J Foyt.

Moving into the 1990's one of the most important concepts was the Citroen Activa 2, which incorporated hydractive suspension with automatic self-levelling

and an active anti-roll system that kept the car on an even keel even during the hardest cornering. Also influential was the Renault Megane of 1991 which was the clear precursor of the production Megane Scenic compact MPV.

Renault was also involved in one of the most madcap concepts of all – the Espace F1 it produced with Matra in 1994. This took the basic form of the Renault Espace MPV but under that relatively familiar skin were the chassis, engine and transmission of a Formula 1 car. This 3.5-litre V10 was capable of accelerating from 0-193 km/h (0-120 mph) in just 6.3 seconds and it went on to an estimated top speed of over 290 km/h (180 mph), even with four passengers on board.

Top Right: *Bertone Stratos*
Bottom Right: *Saturn Curve*

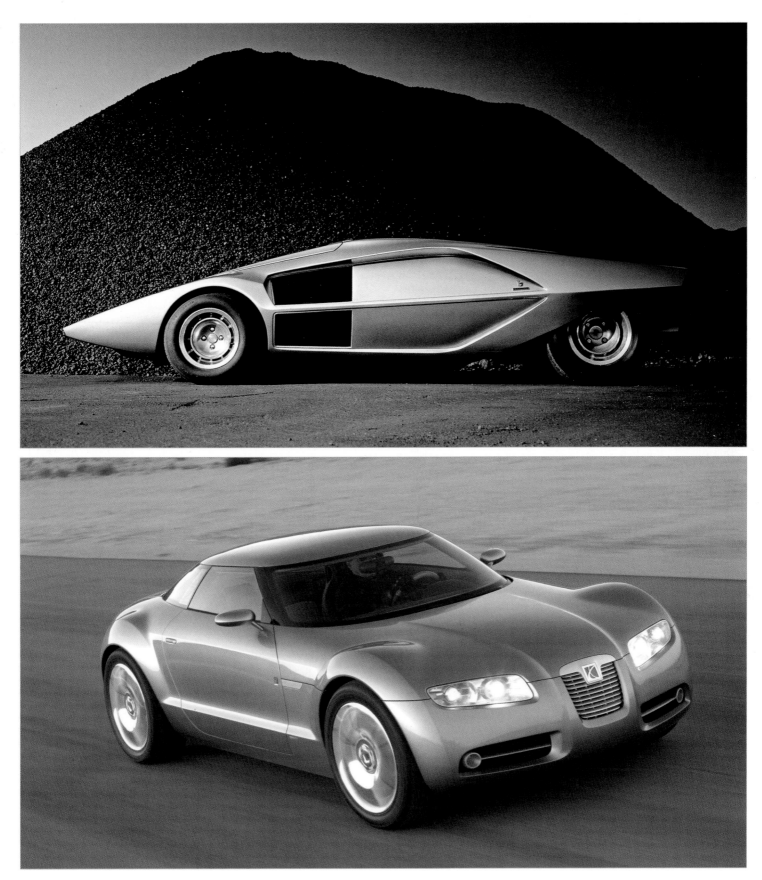

Massive power was also on tap in the Ford GT90 concept of 1995, the mid-engined model that launched Ford's 'new edge design'. It had a 6.0-litre V12 under its carbon fibre bodywork producing a heady 720 bhp.

But 1995 was also the time that environmental concerns became increasingly important, which is why PSA Peugeot-Citroen concentrated less on performance and more on efficiency. It showed its Tulip model that year, which was designed to be part of whole new personal transport infrastructure for urban areas involving small electric cars which would be hired from and returned to one of many stopping points equipped with recharging facilities.

The later 1990's also saw a move to retro styling, a classic example being the Renault Fiftie whose design unashamedly harked back to the Renault 4CV, a model which was then 50 years old.

But others were still looking forward with the 1999 Cadillac Evoq showing the company's new design direction, ItalDesign's Bugatti 18/3 Chiron showing how a grand coupe might look and the Bentley Hunaudieres showing that even a brand such as Bentley could be stretched to a mid-engined GT.

Peugeot's Feline of the following year showed that even a volume car manufacturer could come up with a design that could be a match for Ferrari and Lamborghini, while the Giugiaro-designed Alfa Romeo Brera of 2002 proved that ItalDesign had lost none of its creative powers and that the combination of high power (in this case from a Ferrari-derived V8) and classic Alfa style is still hard to beat.

Historically, very few concept cars ever make it into production. The vast majority were never intended to – they were designed to highlight one or more aspects of safety, performance, practicality, functionality, aerodynamics of just pure visual style. Most fall into one of three categories:

Those that in one way or another hark back to a glorious past and attempt to recapture some aspects of that past in a modern context. Examples might be the Alfa Romeo Nuvola and the Chrysler Atlantic.

Others the manufacturers hope will be well received and will eventually become production cars. Examples are the MINI ACV30, the VW Concept 1 which became the new Beetle and the Audi TT.

And finally there are the massive flights of fancy, the futuristic, way over the top concepts such as the Bertone BAT cars, the spacedream cars of the 1960's and perhaps most vividly the Concept 2096, produced for the British Motor Show in 1996 which has no wheels, no windows and no driver. It is powered by what its designers describe as 'slug drive', which they also cheerfully admit has yet to be invented.

It's madcap designs like that that make motor shows worth attending. Long may they continue to be produced.

Below: *Bugatti 18/3 Chiron*

ABARTH 1600

Technical Specifications	
Abarth 1600	
Year	1969
Engine	1,592cc in-line 4-cylinder
Power	145 bhp @ 7,200 rpm
Torque	Not Quoted
0-62 mph	Not Quoted
Top Speed	240 km/h (146 mph)
ENGINE	
Transmission	6-speed Manual
Drive	Rear-wheel drive
DIMENSIONS	
Length	3800mm
Width	1565mm

The Abarth 1600 is ItalDesign's work from 1969. Using Fiat's in-line 1.6-litre engine and mounting it longitudinally behind the two seats in an aerodynamic body style, the Italian design house succeeded in creating a modern looking sports car with an unusually high top speed for its day.

The pretty little Fiat Abarth 1600 is typical of ItalDesign's work in the late 1960's. Though this concept is based on the Fiat 850 and is fitted with a relatively small in-line engine, the overall design is very similar to that of the V8-powered Alfa Romeo Iguana concept that ItalDesign also produced in 1969.

This concept was one of the earliest pieces of work to emerge from ItalDesign, which was formally set up in 1968, just one year before. The following year would see one of the company's greatest ever commercial successes with the launch of the Alfasud which ItalDesign created as a turnkey project for Alfa Romeo.

ALFA 8C

Technical Specifications	
Alfa Romeo 8C Competizione	
Year	2003
Engine	4244cc V8
Power	400bhp @ 7,000rpm
Torque	325lb.ft @ 4,500rpm
0-62 mph	4.5 seconds.
Top Speed	186 mph / 300 km/h
ENGINE	
Transmission	6 speed Manual
Drive	Rear wheel drive
DIMENSIONS	
Length	4278mm
Width	1900mm

The stunning Alfa coupe first shown at the 2003 Frankfurt Motor Show is a tribute to Alfa's glorious racing past. Back in the 1930's and 1940's the '8C' badge adorned Alfa race and road cars fitted with the new eight cylinder engine designed by Vittorio Jano. As for 'Competizione', that refers to the 6C 2500 Competizione sports coupé driven by Fangio in the 1950 Mille Miglia race.

The Alfa Romeo 8C Competizione is an ultra-modern carbon fibre two-seater whose style harks back to earlier Alfa race cars. For example, the front end resembles the former 33 Coupé Stradale while the rear sports the characteristic round light clusters of the Giulia TZ.

Under the bonnet is a 4.2 litre V8 turbo engine with a volumetric compressor. This classic Alfa V8 delivers over 400 bhp at 7000 rpm and together with a 6-speed manual rear transmission, takes the prototype to a top speed above 300 km/h, accelerating from 0 to 100 kilometres in just 4.5 seconds. But thanks to the engine's massive torque output, the 8C Competizione is a car capable of stunning performance in the real world of everyday roads as well as out on the racetrack.

The 8C Competizione promises both brilliant performance and top notch roadholding and handling thanks to dual wishbone suspension at front and rear. Needless to say, Alfa Romeo chose rear-wheel drive on the 8C Competizione to ensure that this concept is more than just a stunning looker; it also offers the ultimate driving experience.

Technical Specifications	
Alfa Romeo Brera	
Year	2002
Engine	4,000cc V8
Power	402bhp
Torque	400 lb.ft
0-62 mph	Under 6 Sec.
Top Speed	250 km/h (155 mph)
ENGINE	
Transmission	6-speed sequential
Drive	Rear wheel drive
DIMENSIONS	
Length	4388mm
Width	1895mm

The stunning Giugiaro-designed Alfa Romeo Brera was rightly considered the most beautiful car at the 2002 Geneva Motor Show. It combined Alfa's design heritage in a sleek and modern interpretation with the heart of any classic Alfa – a mighty V8 powerplant.

The Brera is based on Maserati Coupé mechanicals so like the Maserati, the concept has its V8 engine at the front and its transmission incorporated into the rear transaxle for better weight balance.

ItalDesign created a new carbon fibre body which is modern yet which is reminiscent of the classic Alfas of old, especially the Montreal. At the front a deep V-grille is flanked by a series of three lights on each side, similar to those on the SZ model of the early 1990's. The rear takes its design cues directly from the 147 and 156 Sport Wagon production cars. The scissor doors with their fixed window glass open via a newly-developed rotary push knob. When rotated outwards, the doors are moved upwards to improve access to the sumptuous interior.

Technical Specifications

Alfa Romeo Kamal	
Year	2003
Engine	3,179cc V6
Power	250 bhp @ 6,200 rpm
Torque	300 Nm @ 4,800 rpm
0-62 mph	Not Quoted
Top Speed	200 km/h (124 mph)
ENGINE	
Transmission	6-speed Sequential
Drive	Four-wheel drive
DIMENSIONS	
Length	4350mm
Width	1860mm

The Alfa Romeo Kamal gets its name from the Arabic meaning 'perfection' and the 'synthesis of opposites'. The concept, revealed at the 2003 Geneva Motor Show, is Alfa's idea of how a crossover sports SUV / MPV might look.

Like all true Alfas, the Kamal is first and foremost a driver's car so it's powered by a 3.2-litre V6 engine mated to a six-speed Selaspeed sequential gearbox which was developed from F1 experience. This concept also has a lower centre of gravity than most SUV's which increases the car's stability at higher speeds.

The doors of the Kamal are unique in that while the front two doors are conventional, the rear doors are side-hinged, activated by an internal mechanism. The rear window is also unusual because it can be opened independently of the tailgate. The tailgate itself has a small 'flap' that can be lowered and extended to the ground to make loading of heavy objects easier.

Technical Specifications	
Alfa Romeo Scighera	
Year	1997
Engine	2,959cc V6
Power	623 bhp @ 6,000 rpm
Torque	560 lb.ft @ 4,000 rpm
0-62 mph	4.9 sec
Top Speed	300 km/h (186 mph)
ENGINE	
Transmission	6-speed Sequential
Drive	Four-wheel drive
DIMENSIONS	
Length	4320mm
Width	1980mm

With 400 bhp on tap, four-wheel drive and a sequential six-speed transmission, the Alfa Romeo Scighera sits firmly in Alfa's long heritage of high-performance grand touring cars. Created by ItalDesign in 1997, it was one of the stars of that year's Geneva Motor Show.

Powered by a modified Alfa V6 from the 164 model, the mid-engined Alfa Romeo Scighera is more than a show car; it is a road-registered fully functional prototype that ItalDesign considered putting into limited production. The engine is mounted longitudinally in front of the rear axle and its power is boosted by twin turbochargers with intercoolers and a further supercharger to ensure plenty of torque even at low engine revs. The four-wheel drive system is an adaptation of Lancia's World Rally Championship winning set up.

To ensure optimum driver comfort, the entire pedal set-up can be adjusted at the touch of an electric button and the steering column is similarly adjustable.

Technical Specifications	
Alfa Romeo Visconti	
Year	2004
Engine	3,200cc V6
Power	405bhp @ 6,000rpm
Torque	502lb.ft @ 2,000rpm
0-62 mph	Not Quoted.
Top Speed	Not Quoted
ENGINE	
Transmission	6 speed Auto
Drive	Four wheel drive
DIMENSIONS	
Length	4955mm
Width	1896mm

The Alfa Romeo Visconti is Giorgio Giugiaro's idea of how a flagship Alfa should look. It's not a traditional three-box saloon more of a two-box sports car featuring a downward sloping tail. The name Visconti refers to the ancient Visconti Milanese family whose coat of arms was adopted as the Alfa Romeo marque.

This is not Giugiaro's first experiment with two-box architecture – back in 1993 his Bugatti EB112 was an earlier example of a two-box sports sedan. The Visconti is based on Alfa's premium platform, developed for the production Alfa Romeo 156 range but in this case the wheelbase has been lengthened and the finiahsed product is almost five metres long. Under the bonnet is a powerful 405bhp bi-turbo petrol V6 engine mated to a six-speed automatic gearbox. Permanent four wheel drive is adopted for ultimate stability and this is combined with a pneumatic suspension system that allows the ride height to be adjusted according to speed and road conditions..

ASTON MARTIN 20-20

Based on the Aston Martin DB7, the ItalDesign Aston Martin Twenty Twenty is a concept that investigates the use of space frame technology combined with body panels which are bolted or glued to the bearing structure, thus allowing customization at low cost.

The Aston Martin 20-20 is a 2+2 seater whose rear seats can be removed when not required. Based on the Aston Martin DB7 Vantage coupe, the 20-20 uses the production V12 engine and drive train and incorporates a see-through bonnet to ensure the magnificent power unit remains on full display.

The concept features grey carbon fibre body panels stretched between the extruded aluminium frame which remains on show at all times. Though the car is a drivable prototype, it was never put into production. As to the name, 20-20 refers to perfect vision.

Technical Specifications

Aston Martin 20-20

Year	2001
Engine	5,935cc V12
Power	500 bhp @ 6,000 rpm
Torque	Not Quoted
0-62 mph	4.6 sec
Top Speed	300 km/h (186 mph)
ENGINE	
Transmission	6-speed Manual
Drive	Rear wheel drive
DIMENSIONS	
Length	4455mm
Width	1899mm

Technical Specifications

Audi Asgard	
Year	1988
Engine	2,226cc in-line 5-cylinder
Power	200 bhp @ 6,200 rpm
Torque	Not Quoted
0-62 mph	Not Quoted
Top Speed	Not Quoted
ENGINE	
Transmission	5-speed Manual
Drive	Four-wheel drive
DIMENSIONS	
Length	4419mm
Width	4419mm

The Audi Asgard was one of three related concepts all based around Audi's turbocharged 5-cylinder 2.2-litre engine and created by ItalDesign in 1988. This one is a sleek 8-seater MPV which boasts impressive interior space despite its mid-engined layout.

I t's perhaps a surprise to find Audi's World Rally Championship winning powertrain and four-wheel drive system on an MPV, but part of ItalDesign's purpose with the Asgard was to see how a single basic structure could be adapted for different purposes.

While the other related concepts – the Aztec and the Aspid – were both two-seat sports cars with different interchangeable body panels to differentiate between them, the Asgard was a styling concept that revealed how elegant even a comparatively large MPV vehicle could be, without any loss of interior practicality and flexibility.

Technical Specifications	
Audi Aspid	
Year	1988
Engine	2,226cc in-line 5-cylinder
Power	200 bhp @ 6,200 rpm
Torque	Not Quoted
0-62 mph	Not Quoted
Top Speed	Not Quoted
ENGINE	
Transmission	5-speed Manual
Drive	Four-wheel drive
DIMENSIONS	
Length	4267mm
Width	1981mm

ItalDesign's Audi Aspid was never any more than a pure styling concept whose aim was to show how a model such as the Audi Aztec could be converted easily and at relatively low cost into a different mid-engined sports car.

While the Audi Aztec upon which the Aspid is based had two separate cockpits for the driver and passenger, the Aspid had a single cabin accessed via two conventional doors and a glass dome windscreen that tilted forwards. Behind a partially transparent rear engine cover was a space for luggage. There was also a smaller luggage compartment under the short front bonnet.

Like the Aztec, the Aspid is based on Audi's permanent four-wheel drive Quattro platform and is powered by the Audi 2.2-litre turbocharged 2.2-litre engine.

AUDI AVUS QUATTRO

The Audi Avus Quattro caused a sensation when unveiled at the 1991 Frankfurt Motor Show. Not only did it have stunning lines – the work of J Mays – but it was also powered by an astonishing 509 bhp 60-valve W12 engine.

The Audi Avus Quattro is a deliberate reminder of the great Auto Union race cars and record breakers of the 1930's, which is why, like those great classics, this concept is finished in unpainted aluminium.

The W12 engine is a completely new departure, however, and owes nothing to Audi's or Auto union's heritage. The cylinders are arranged in three banks of four cylinders which results in a compact and short power unit which is mid-mounted and drives all four wheels via Audi's Quattro system. Performance is at supercar levels, with a top speed of 341 km/h (212 mph) and acceleration from 0-62 mph I under three seconds.

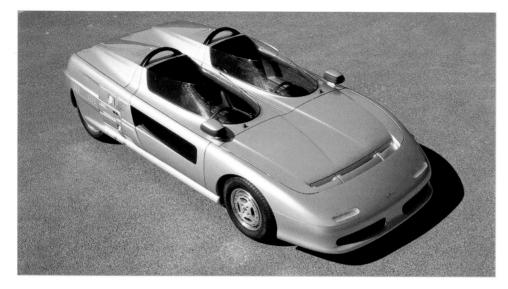

Technical Specifications

Audi Aztec

Year	1988
Engine	2,226cc in-line 5-cylinder
Power	250 bhp @ 6,200 rpm
Torque	Not Quoted
0-62 mph	6.5 sec
Top Speed	241 km/h (150 mph)
ENGINE	
Transmission	5-speed Manual
Drive	Four-wheel drive
DIMENSIONS	
Length	4269mm
Width	1981mm

Unlike the other related concepts (Aspid and Asgard) ItalDesign's Audi Aztec was a fully engineered prototype that actually went into limited production with some 255 examples being produced. Unveiled at the 1988 Turin Motor Show it was liked so much by the Japanese company Compakt that it commissioned a production run.

Entry to the Aztec was via a code entered on a key pad, rather than with a conventional key. Though the original Aztec concept could be driven from either of the two separate front cockpits, once in production there was just a single steering wheel. But the driver and passenger still communicated via headsets connected to an intercom system.

In production the chassis and bodies were built in Italy then shipped to Germany for a tuned Audi 5-cylinder turbocharged engine to be fitted. The four-wheel drive system was an adaptation of the Lancia Integrale's components. The body was constructed of steel, carbon fibre and aluminium.

AUDI LE MANS

Audi's Le Mans Quattro concept clearly derives from Audi's successes on the race tracks and particularly from the company's successive wins at Le Mans in 2000, 2001 and 2002. This is a high-performance roadgoing sports car which has inherited the genes of the Audi R8 track car.

This soul of the Le Mans Quattro concept is a twin-turbocharged V10 engine producing massive power and high torque. This is mated to a sequential-shift 6-speed transmission operated by steering-wheel mounted paddle shifts; an electro-hydraulic system means no clutch pedal is required. The concept is based on Audi's aluminium space frame technology with a lightweight outer skin made of aluminium and carbon fibre resulting in a total weight of just 1530kg. The combination of massive power and light weight results in a theoretical top speed of 214 mph (345 km/h), but this is electronically limited to 155 mph (250 km/h). To match the performance, the Le Mans Quattro is fitted with ceramic brakes incorporating eight-piston fixed callipers.

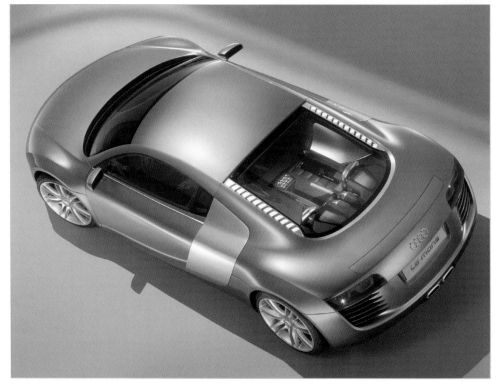

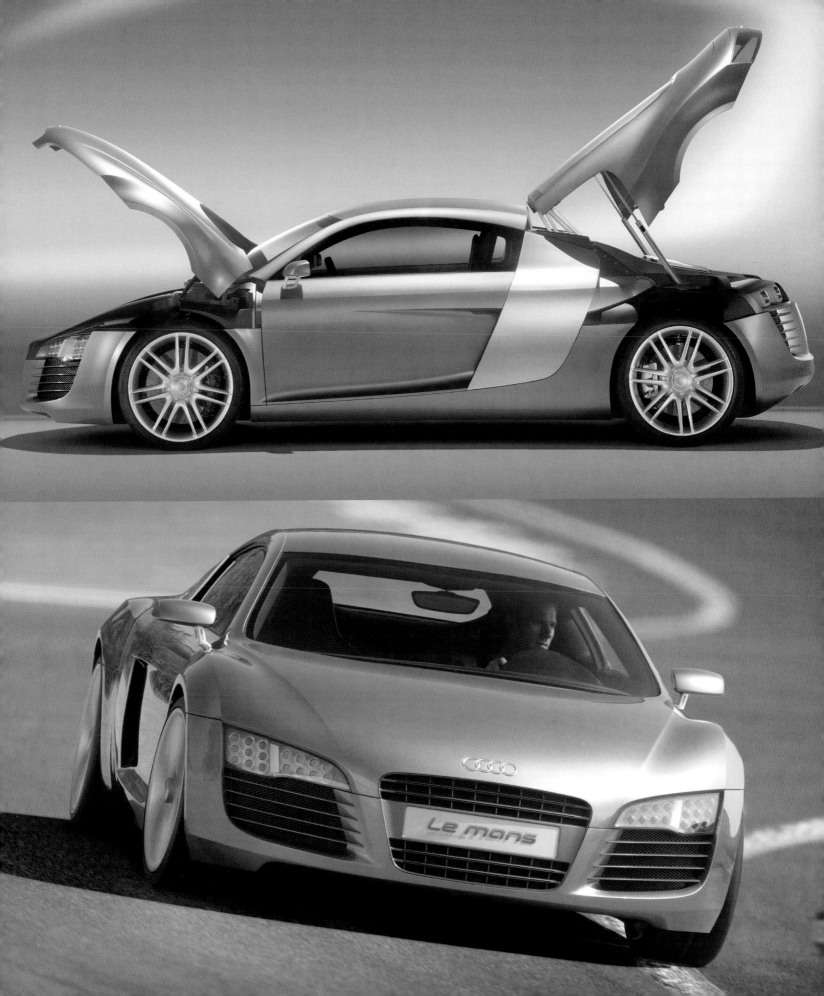

AUDI RSQ

Technical Specifications	
Audi RSQ	
Year	2004
Engine	Not quoted
Power	Not quoted
Torque	Not quoted
0-62 mph	Not quoted
Top Speed	Not quoted
ENGINE	
Transmission	Not quoted
Drive	Not quoted
DIMENSIONS	
Length	Not quoted
Width	Not quoted

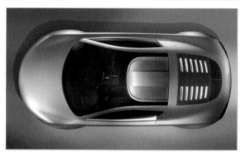

The Audi RSQ is a concept of what an Audi sports car might look like in the year 2035. It was created for the film 'I, Robot' starring Will Smith, and is seen in the movie being raced by Smith around the streets of Chicago.

The Audi RSQ takes product placement to a whole new level. It's a mid-engined sports car that runs not on wheels but on spheres. It's operated by the Chicago police department and is used by homicide detective Will Smith to help solve a mystery that could have extreme consequences for the human race.

The Audi RSQ displays clear Audi design language though its two doors, which are hinged on the C-pillars and open like a butterfly's wings, are unlikely ever to see production. This is the first time that Audi has created a concept car specifically for a movie.

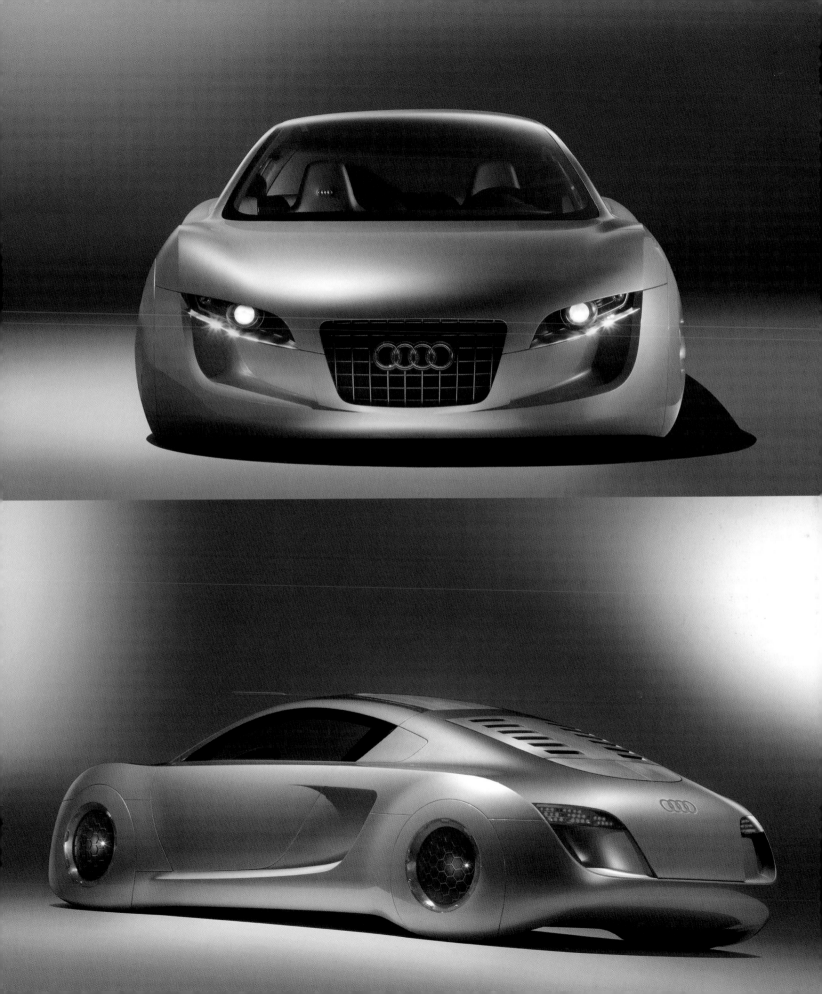

BERTONE PORSCHE KARISMA

Technical Specifications	
Bertone Porsche Karisma	
Year	1994
Engine	3,600cc horizontally-opposed 6-cylinder
Power	272 bhp @ 6,100 rpm
Torque	Not Quoted
0-62 mph	Not Quoted
Top Speed	Not Quoted
ENGINE	
Transmission	6-speed Manual
Drive	Rear-wheel drive
DIMENSIONS	
Length	4520mm
Width	1860mm

The Porsche Karisma was created by Bertone to investigate the possibility of producing a comfortable and practical four-seater performance car with a rear engine. It was based on a Porsche 911 chassis and mechanicals and undoubtedly succeeded in its design brief.

This was not Bertone's first partnership with Porsche. Back in 1966 the Italian design house produced a Porsche 911 Roadster for one of Porsche's American dealerships and unveiled it at the Geneva Motor Show before it was shipped to the States.

Nearly 20 years later, the Porsche 911 was still in production and Bertone again looked to that iconic car as a base for a new concept. This time he chose to create a luxury four-seat high-performance saloon. The main features are its deep swage lines running along the wings, its transparent roof and its large gull-wing doors incorporating the whole sills, an idea first proposed on the 1967 Lamborghini Marzal concept. Also interesting is the glazed panel showing the engine compartment in all its glory.

BERTONE JET2

Technical Specifications

Bertone Jet 2	
Year	2005
Engine	5,935cc V8
Power	528bhp @ 7,000rpm
Torque	426 lb.ft @ 5,800rpm
0-62 mph	4.8 sec (est.)
Top Speed	190 mph (306 km/h) (est.)
ENGINE	
Transmission	6 speed Automatic
Drive	Rear wheel drive
DIMENSIONS	
Length	4675mm
Width	1930mm

The Bertone Jet 2 is perhaps the ultimate custom-built vehicle. Like a made to measure suit from a great tailor, this is a one-off based on a prestigious production vehicle – in this case the Aston Martin Vanquish. The name is a tribute to the Aston Martin Jet created by Nuccio Bertone in 1961, based on the DB4 GT.

The Bertone Jet 2 has the same mechanical layout and floorpan structure as the standard Aston Martin Vanquish, though the floorpan has been lengthened by 2100 mm to allow two rear seats to the added. While it's the same under the skin as the standard Vanquish, Jet 2's body is entirely new. This is Bertone's modern-day concept which harks back to the long history of Italian coachbuilders. It is also an example of how Bertone could help small volume manufacturers like Aston Martin to diversify their own range by offering bespoke "custom-built' vehicles just as they did in the 1950's and 1960's.

What is important in this concept is that it uses the maximum number of components fro the original car, so costs are kept within reasonable limits. The Jet 2 also maintains all the structural specifications of the original vehicle so there is no compromise on safety or performance.

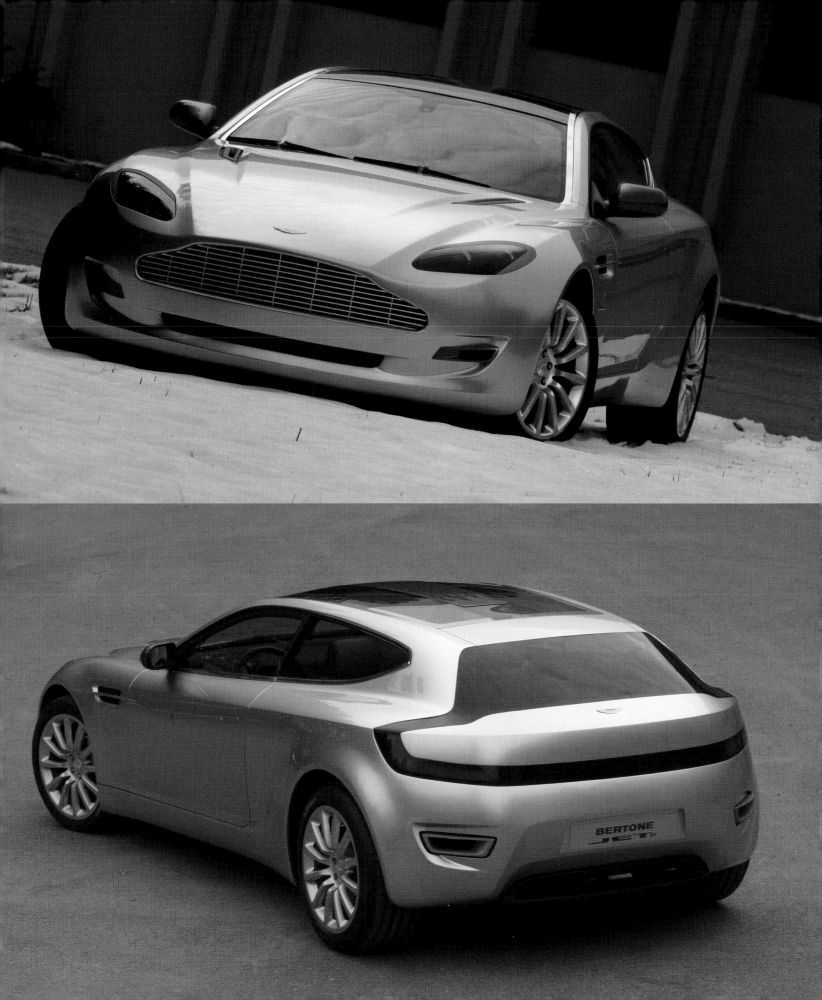

BIZZARINI MANTA

The Bizzarini Manta was one of the most influential concept cars of the 1960's, partly because it was the very first concept car that Giorgetto Giugiaro styled following the foundation of ItalDesign; but also because of its bold lines and radical three-abreast seating with the driver (and steering wheel) in the middle.

The sleek and elegant Bizzarini Manta was first unveiled on ItalDesign's stand at the Turin Motor Show in 1968. The one-box mid-engined GT was based upon the tubular chassis of the Bizzarini P538 Spyder with a Chevrolet V8 mounted behind the passenger cabin. It featured three abreast seating, though unlike the later McLaren F1 which had the driver sitting slightly ahead of the passengers to create more shoulder room, the centrally positioned Manta driver sat side by side with the two passengers which resulted in a tight squeeze in the cabin. From a design point of view the Manta was typical late 1960's, with sharp angular lines and a profusion of strakes and vents. Interestingly, it was one of the earliest examples of cab-forward architecture.

Sadly, the publicity that ItalDesign's Manta provided for the small Italian

manufacturer Bizzarini didn't do much good. The production P538 was not a success and Bizzarini operations were closed down in 1969 though later another version of the P538, the Varedo was developed for Iso in 1972. It never made it into production.

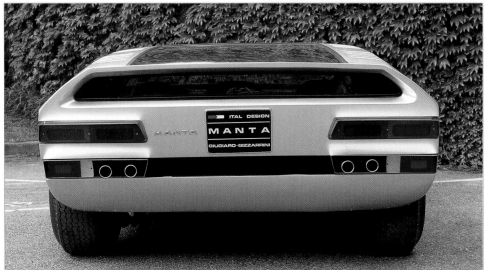

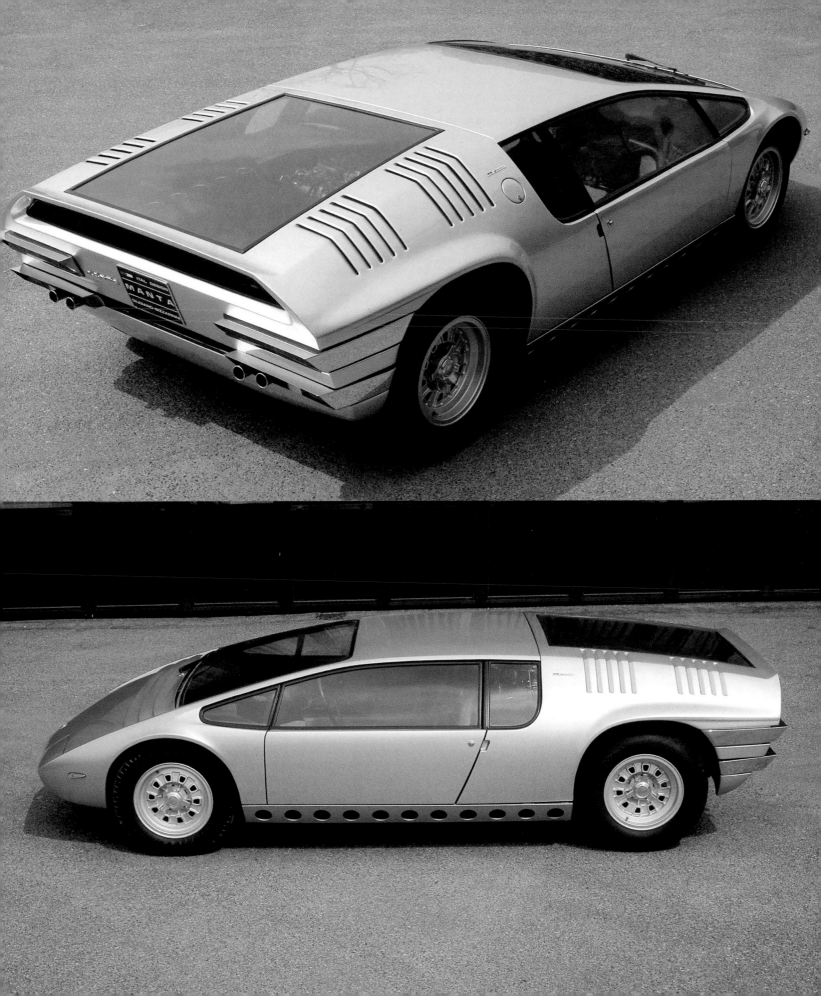

BMW CS1

Technical Specifications	
BMW CS1	
Year	2002
Engine	1,796cc in-line 4-cylinder
Power	115 bhp @ 5,500 rpm
Torque	129 lb.ft. @ 3,750 rpm
0-62 mph	Not quoted
Top Speed	Not quoted
ENGINE	
Transmission	5 speed Automatic
Drive	Rear wheel drive
DIMENSIONS	
Length	Not quoted
Width	Not quoted

The four-seater BMW CS1 convertible concept car is clearly a BMW that demonstrates all the main design features of the brand, but in this case those brand values are interpreted in such as way as to appeal more to a younger and more innovative audience.

The design of the CS1 combines agility with a powerful dynamism with its broad shoulder line, flowing side sills and muscular wheels with their massive and clearly visible brakes. A high rising front end with dual headlights and a twin kidney grille gives the CS1 a dynamic and watchful facewhile short overhangs front and rear are typical of BMW.

Inside the cockpit there's a philosophy of light elegance. There are no opulent or bulky components and instead the designers tried to conjure up the feeling of the worlds of fashion and modern architecture. Both classic and modern materials are utilized and one innovation is the use of transparent gel pads in the seat bottoms to ensure maximum comfort even on long journeys.

BMW Nazca C2

Technical Specifications	
BMW Nazca C2	
Year	1991
Engine	5660cc V12
Power	380bhp @ 5,300rpm
Torque	Not quoted
0-62 mph	Not quoted
Top Speed	Not quoted
ENGINE	
Transmission	5 speed Manual
Drive	Rear wheel drive
DIMENSIONS	
Length	4395mm
Width	2085mm

Little more than six months after the BMW Nazca M12 was unveiled at the Geneva Show an even sportier version of the concept was revealed at the Tokyo Motor Show in October 1991. The Nazca C2, again produced by ItalDesign now boasted an even more powerful BMW V12 engine together with a subtly reworked body.

The BMW Nazca C2 has exactly the same composite monocoque chassis under its skin as the earlier Nazca M12. It also retains the mid-engine layout and two-door coupe configuration. But a larger and more powerful 5.6-litre Alpina BMW V12 replaces the earlier 5.0-litre unit. Performance figures for this model were never officially revealed, but it's fair to assume that the C2 could reach 0-62mph in around 4.0 seconds and had a top speed of at least 195 mph / 314 km/h.

Styling changes, especially at the front and rear, give the Nazca C2 a more aggressive and purposeful look and the point of the C2 exercise was to demonstrate how easily a model like this can be modified without affecting its basic structure. Apparently ItalDesign took orders from around 50 potential buyers and seriously considered a short production run. However, this would have required the support of BMW and even though ItalDesign had the capability – it had produced the M1 for BMW – the project never got off the ground.

BMW Nazca C2 Spider	
Year	1991
Engine	5660cc V12
Power	380bhp @ 5,300rpm
Torque	Not quoted
0-62 mph	Not quoted
Top Speed	Not quoted
ENGINE	
Transmission	5 speed Manual
Drive	Rear wheel drive
DIMENSIONS	
Length	4395mm
Width	2085mm

A third BMW Nazca prototype was wheeled out at the prestigious Monaco Grand Prix in May 1993. The C2 Spider shared the mechanicals and running gear of the coupe C2 but in the meantime had lost both its roof and its engine cover, thus revealing the aluminium V12 cylinder heads to the onlooking world.

The BMW Nazca C2 Spider was the third and last embodiment of the Nazca project and in many ways it was the most successful. The magnificent Alpina BMW V12 engine was on show beneath a transparent rear cover and the spider construction added another element to the overall design. Interestingly, the colour of the concept car was changed shortly after its unveiling at the Monaco grand prix. There, the Nazca C2 Spider was grey, as the two previous Nazca concepts had been. But the Spider later re-appeared in a bright red livery, a colour chosen by Fabrizio Giugiaro "for aesthetic reasons".

The C2 Spider was ItalDesign's third working of the Nazca concept which, if nothing else, generated enormous worldwide publicity for the firm. Just as importantly, it proved ItalDesign's ability to design and build a world-class sports chassis that could be adapted quickly and relatively inexpensively to take different body configurations.

BMW Nazca M12

Technical Specifications	
BMW Nazca M12	
Year	1991
Engine	4988cc V12
Power	300bhp @ 5,200rpm
Torque	332 lb.ft @ 4,100
0-62 mph	4.5 seconds
Top Speed	189mph / 304 km/h
ENGINE	
Transmission	5 speed Manual
Drive	Rear wheel drive
DIMENSIONS	
Length	4365mm
Width	1990mm

The stunning BMW Nazca M12 came about when ItalDesign decided to build an in-house sports car. The plan for 1991 had been to turn the 1990 Bugatti ID90 clay model into a running prototype but instead father and son Giorgio and Fabrizio Giugiaro set about the more ambitious task of creating a specific chassis and suspension system. In the end the only parts bought off the shelf were the BMW V12 engine and ZF transmission; all the rest was ItalDesign's work.

In developing the Nazca M12, Giorgio Giugiaro concentrated on the shape and appearance while son Fabrizio took responsibility for the vehicle's construction and mechanical layout. This layout was taken directly from Group C race car experience, being a sophisticated carbon fibre structure with a load-bearing monocoque and magnesium rear sub-chassis.

First revealed at the 1991 Geneva Motor Show, the Nazca M12 with its low glass cabin didn't just look good, it was also extremely aerodynamic with a Cd of just 0.26. There was talk at the time that this might become a successor to BMW's limited production M1 roadster because the car was designed from the outset for

low-volume production. In the end, the powers that be at BMW chose not to beat a path to ItalDesign's door, which is a shame because only very rarely does such a beautiful, elegant and stunningly quick sports car make an appearance.

BMW X-Coupe

Technical Specifications	
BMW X-Coupé	
Year	2001
Engine	3,000cc in-line 6-cylinder
Power	184 bhp
Torque	332 lb.ft.
0-62 mph	Not quoted
Top Speed	125 mph (201 km/h)
ENGINE	
Transmission	5 speed Automatic
Drive	Four wheel drive
DIMENSIONS	
Length	4579mm
Width	1869mm

BMW's X-Coupé concept was a surprise debut at the 2001 Detroit Show. Dramatically different to anything that BMW had created before, the concept was intended both to challenge traditional design theory and also to show a new stylistic direction for BMW production cars.

Based on a BMW X5 4x4 chassis, the X-Coupé concept is powered by a 3.0-litre turbodiesel engine. A 5-speed automatic transmission takes drive to all four wheels, so the X-Coupé has a degree of off-road cabability as well as fine road manners.

In terms of design, the concept introduces what BMW calls Flame Surfacing which body surfaces the freedom to turn in on themselves and create a series of concave and convex design lines. These can be seen on the doors, the dash and on the top of the front wings where the bodywork has an unusual concave shape. Also interesting are the assymetrical rear lights and assymetrical tailgate in which almost the entire rear section opens by tilting rearward, revealing the cargo space and rear seats. The absence of a C pillar on the passenger window side allows the front window to merge seamlessly into the rear window, allowing cargo and passengers entering and exiting from the curb very easy access.

Technical Specifications	
Bugatti EB112	
Year	1993
Engine	6000cc V12
Power	455 bhp @ 6,300 rpm
Torque	434 lb.ft @ 3,000 rpm
0-62 mph	Not quoted
Top Speed	Not quoted
ENGINE	
Transmission	6 speed Manual
Drive	Four-wheel drive
DIMENSIONS	
Length	5070mm
Width	1960mm

The Bugatti EB112 was never intended as a concept, but as a limited-run production car. Unveiled at the Geneva Show in March 1993, the plan was to produce 300 examples which would go on sale in spring 1995. Production plans were shelved and the EB112 remained a dream.

When Bugatti Automobili filed for bankruptcy in 1994, plans to produce the EB112 were swiftly halted. Which is a shame because on paper it looked to have been a stunning Grand Tourer, capable of carrying five passengers at high speeds over long distances. The two-box grand touring saloon was developed by ItalDesign around Bugatti's own 6-litre V12 engine that produced what at that time was a massive 455bhp but work came to a halt when ItalDesign's bills stopped being paid.

Its style – particularly its radiator grille and its central roof rib – recalled the famous Bugatti Atlantic of the 1930's. Inside the cabin was a heady combination of leather and wood, with both driver and front seat passenger sitting in their own cockpit space separated by a massive central transmission tunnel – necessary to accommodate a gearbox capable of handling over 434 lb.ft. of torque.

Bugatti EB118

When Bugatti Automobili went into bankruptcy in 1994 the pieces of the company were picked up by Volkswagen Group. And one of the first things VW did was to ask ItalDesign – which had produced the EB112 – to revive the Bugatti Grand Touring concept. The result was the EB118, first revealed at the Paris Show in 1998.

Underneath the svelte bodywork of the EB118 is a revolutionary – some would say bizarre – W18 engine. It has eighteen cylinders in three banks, displaces 6.3-litres and pushes out some 555bhp. Partly to emphasise the power of the engine and partly to make it physically fit under the bonnet, the EB118 has a bulging shape which rises over the wings and, following the style of both the Bugatti Atlantic of the 1930's and the earlier EB112, it has a distinct ridge over the roof. In this case the ridge extends over the bonnet and down the boot too.

The interior of the EB118 follows an Art Deco theme with extensive use of suede materials on the dashboard, seats and fascia. It's not to everyone's taste, but then even were this monster ever to have been put into production, not everyone would have been able to afford it.

BUGATTI EB218

Technical Specifications	
Bugatti EB218	
Year	1999
Engine	6255cc W18
Power	555 bhp @ 6,300 rpm
Torque	479 lb.ft @ 4,000rpm
0-62 mph	Not quoted
Top Speed	Not quoted
ENGINE	
Transmission	5 speed Automatic
Drive	Four-wheel drive
DIMENSIONS	
Length	5375mm
Width	1990mm

For the Geneva Show 1999 Bugatti, now under the auspices of the Volkswagen Group, produced yet another Grand Tourer design, and one which was promised for production. Like the earlier EB118, the EB218 was powered by a massive W18 6.3-litre engine.

The EB218 was intended for production and had a sparkling specification. Aluminium spaceframe technology was used for its body, while permanent four-wheel drive and aluminium multi-link suspension promised impressive driving dynamics and excellent traction. As for the engine, the three banks of six cylinders comprising the W18 engine featured direct injection technology for maximum combustion efficiency.

Though the design followed the earlier EB118, the 118's coupe style has been transformed into a full saloon body. What was retained was the very distinctive Bugatti grille and ridge over the bonnet, roof and boot lid. In the cabin, oval instruments are framed in leather and specification included satellite navigation and telephone equipped for satellite reception. A TV and video is integrated into the rear. Also notable was a motorised loading tray in the boot to convey luggage into the boot space.

A Bugatti saloon has still not gone on sale, so the EB218 remains nothing more than an interesting historical concept.

Technical Specifications

Bugatti ID90	
Year	1990
Engine	3,498cc V12
Power	Not quoted
Torque	Not quoted
0-62 mph	Not quoted
Top Speed	Not quoted
ENGINE	
Transmission	Not quoted
Drive	Four wheel drive
DIMENSIONS	
Length	4089mm
Width	1828mm

The Bugatti ID90 was ItalDesign's idea of what a modern Bugatti supercar might look like. It was based around a quad-turbocharged V12 engine and presented an idea of what a forthcoming mid-engined Bugatti spors car might be. In the event, the project never went further than the show model unveiled at Turin in 1990.

The Bugatti ID90, one of Giorgetto Giugiaro's finest creations, is widely held to be the best looking of all the many Bugatti concepts and prototypes that were built during the 1990's. But this mid-engined supercar was never to make it anywhere near production. In 1991 Bugatti rights were bought by Romano Artioli and he commissioned the EB110 model in 1991. Giugiaro was again involved in 1993 with the EB112 in 1993 which ItalDesign built under commission from Artioli. Sadly Artioli's business went into liquidation in 1995.

Though only a clay model, Giugiaro's ID90 revealed some interesting concepts, not least the fully glazed and apparently pillarless windscreen, roof and rear screen panels. The mid-mounted longitudinal V12 engine was cooled via massive rear strakes which combined to form a broad rear spoiler.

BUICK BENGAL

Technical Specifications

Buick Bengal	
Year	2001
Engine	3,350cc V6
Power	250bhp
Torque	240 lb.ft
0-62 mph	Not Quoted
Top Speed	Not Quoted
ENGINE	
Transmission	6-speed Automatic
Drive	Front Wheel Drive
DIMENSIONS	
Length	4445mm
Width	1867mm

The Buick Bengal was named Best Concept of all those shown at the Paris, Detroit and Geneva Motor Shows of 2001 by Autoweek Magazine. It looks like a two-seat convertible but it actually has a third door behind the driver's door that allows space for two more passengers of golf bags.

The most striking thing about the interior of the 2001 Buick Bengal concept car is the absence of any controls or gauges. This car will respond to verbal instructions from the driver, thanks to a partnership between Visteon Corporation and General Motors which demonstrates technology that will blend safety, personalization, comfort and convenience. The driver can issue more than 118 commands to the car, operating the headlights, wipers, heating system, sound system, convertible top, on-board navigation, seat adjustments and cruise control.

The voice control system eliminates the need for controls and displays traditionally found on an instrument panel. In turn, the Bengal's dashboard has become a large flat-panel speaker from NXT, with superior sound reproduction in an unobtrusive package.

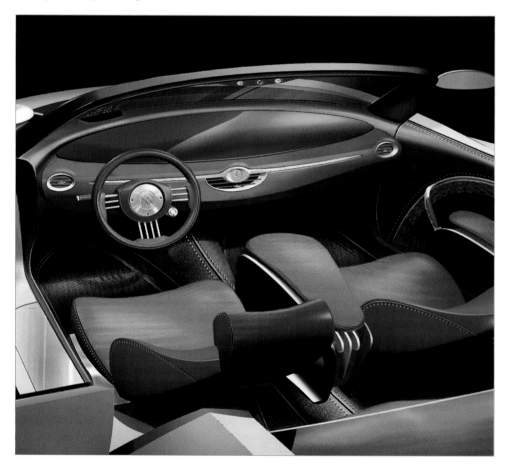

BUICK LaCROSSE

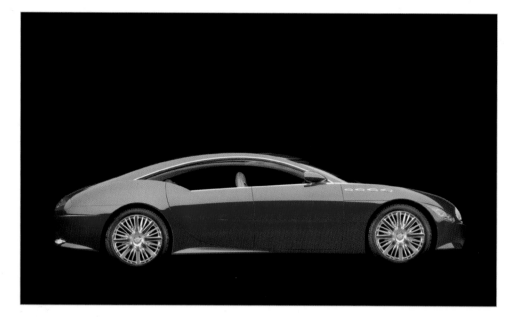

Technical Specifications	
Buick LaCrosse	
Year	2000
Engine	4,200cc V8
Power	265bhp @ 5,600 rpm
Torque	240 lb.ft
0-62 mph	Not Quoted
Top Speed	Not Quoted
ENGINE	
Transmission	6-speed Automatic
Drive	Front-wheel drive
DIMENSIONS	
Length	5194mm
Width	1953mm

Buick 's LaCrosse combines the grace of a premium family saloon with the carrying capacity of a small pick-up truck. In its primary mode, it's a four-door saloon but it can be transformed into a pick-up with a 40 by 40 inch open bed for transporting bulky items.

In addition to the pick-up bed – which can actually be extended to 80 inches in length with the rear seats folded down – there's secure storage for custom-fitted luggage inside a 5.1 cubic foot underfloor compartment accessible through a double-hinged panel. So the Buick LaCrosse is geared to transport two people in comfort with all the luggage and recreational gear they might need for a weekend away.

The interior is not only one of the roomiest Buicks ever, but also one of the most inviting, thanks to a simple, uncomplicated approach to the design. A 'jog shuttle' (a mushroom shaped combination mouse and joy stick) is used to control the transmission, navigation, climate control and audio equipment.

BUICK LeSabre

Technical Specifications	
Buick LeSabre	
Year	1951
Engine	3,533cc V8
Power	335bhp @ 5,200rpm
Torque	380lb.ft @ 3,650
0-62 mph	Not quoted
Top Speed	Not quoted
ENGINE	
Transmission	4 speed Automatic
Drive	Rear wheel drive
DIMENSIONS	
Length	5128mm
Width	2014mm

The 1950 Buick LeSabre is one of the automotive industry's best known and most famous concept cars. Designed by GM's Harley J. Earl, the LeSabre was used by him for his everyday transport for many years after the concept was first unveiled in Chicago.

The Buick LeSabre was critically important in styling terms because it was one of the very first attempts to incorporate aircraft styling into automotive design. In a sense it was a living preview of the aircraft styling that became a feature of American car design in the later 1950's. Even its name derived from a fighter aircraft. But underneath the radical skin the LeSabre also offered some technological breakthroughs including a dual petrol and alcohol fuel system and a moisture sensor that automatically raised the convertible hood top if it started to rain while the car was parked.

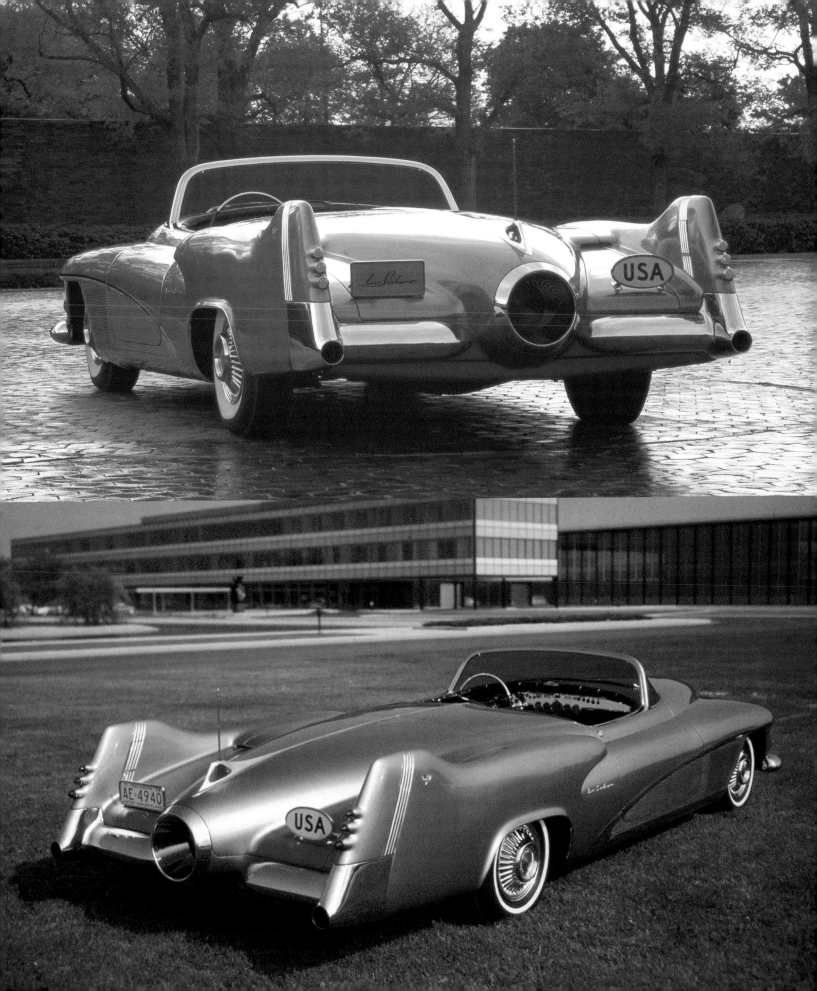

BUICK Y-JOB

Technical Specifications	
Buick Y-Job	
Year	1938
Engine	5,245cc in-line 8-cylinder
Power	141 bhp
Torque	Not Quoted
0-62 mph	Not Quoted
Top Speed	Not Quoted
ENGINE	
Transmission	6-speed Automatic
Drive	Rear-wheel drive
DIMENSIONS	
Length	5293mm
Width	1889mm

The Buick Y-Job is probably the first concept car ever produced. Built in 1938 it had concealed headlights and an electrical top which was concealed under a metal cover when opened up.

This "Dream Car" was a long, low convertible based on the Buick Roadmaster saloon. It was designed by George Snyder under the direction of Harley J Earl and in fact Earl used the car as his personal transport for some years after it was produced in 1938. One of this concept's innovations was the vertical-bar treatment of the grille which for years after became the trademark of Buick cars.

The innovative retractable headlights were not a very practical proposition at that time and when production of Buick cars resumed after the Second World War, they were replaced by a more conventional lighting system.

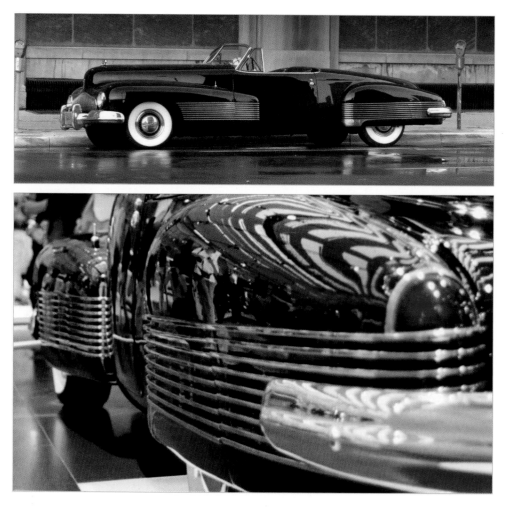

Technical Specifications	
Cadillac IMAJ	
Year	2000
Engine	4,200cc V8
Power	425bhp @ 6,400rpm
Torque	400 lb.ft @ 4,000 rpm
0-62 mph	Not Quoted
Top Speed	160 km/h (100mph) (Est.)
ENGINE	
Transmission	5-speed Automatic
Drive	Four-wheel drive
DIMENSIONS	
Length	5100mm
Width	1900mm

First revealed at the 2000 Geneva Motor Show, the Cadillac IMAJ is a direct descendant of the earlier Evoq concept roadster. In this instance, the concept is for an all-wheel drive luxury sedan that combines exhilarating performance with unprecendted technological applications.

The Cadillac IMAJ is powered by a revised version of GM's supercharged Northstar B8 engine that features a liquid-to-air intercooler and continuously variable valve timing to produce 425bhp. This power is fed to all four wheels through an all-new five-speed automatic transmission.

New technologies include Night Vision which works both back and front to enhance the driver's vision. Obstacle alert sensors and rear vision cameras which replace the mirrors also enhance rearward visibility. A head-up display, shift-by-wire gear selection and adaptive cruise control are all part of the impressive specification.

Technical Specifications	
Cadillac Vizon	
Year	2001
Engine	4,200cc V8
Power	300bhp
Torque	300 lb.ft
0-62 mph	Not Quoted
Top Speed	Not Quoted
ENGINE	
Transmission	5-speed Automatic
Drive	Four-wheel drive
DIMENSIONS	
Length	4826mm
Width	1800mm

The Cadillac Vizon fits somewhere into the gap between the sports utility vehicle and the sporty estate car. Though it's a concept that difficult to pigeon-hole, its sharp-edged styling ensures it can't be mistaken for anything other than a Cadillac.

In creating the Cadillac Vizon, the designers opted for simple, clean surfaces that are sheer and sharp, paying homage to the concept that 'less is more'. It's an alternative to a sports utility vehicle with a more car-like driving experience. Power comes from GM's 4.2-litre Northstar V8 mated to a five-speed automatic transmission. Suspension height can be altered for different road and load conditions.

Like the Cadillac Evoq and Imaj concept cars that preceded it, the Vizon unites the best qualities of several different kinds of vehicle. Inside the four passengers have individually heated and cooled seats and have access to DVD and built-in video screens. A centre console extends the whole length of the car's interior, so skis and other long items can be carried.

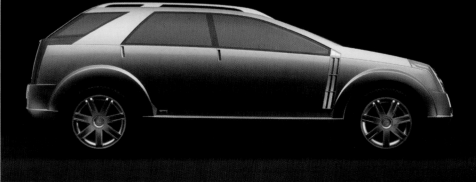

CHEVROLET BORREGO

Technical Specifications	
Chevrolet Borrego	
Year	2001
Engine	2,500cc horizontally opp four-cylinder
Power	250bhp
Torque	240 lb.ft
0-62 mph	Not Quoted
Top Speed	Not Quoted
ENGINE	
Transmission	5-speed Manual
Drive	Four-wheel drive
DIMENSIONS	
Length	4273mm
Width	1820mm

Like the Pontiac Rev which appeared the same year, the 2001 Chevrolet Borrego takes the rally car as its starting point. Its aim is to offer a comfortable family or commuting vehicle during the week with the ability to offer sporty off-road performance at weekends.

The style of the Chevy Borrego is influenced by rally cars in general and Baja racers in particular. The car's sporty, swept-back look and athletic stance derives both from international rally cars but also from the customized pick-up culture of California. Practical features include an on-board air compressor and a pressurized water tank. The air hose can be used to clean the interior or inflate outdoor equipment while the pressurized tank can provide a shower at the end of a hard day's off-roading.

The Borrego's powertrain is based on the Subaru four-wheel drive system that has enjoyed such success in international rallying. GM owns 20% of the Japanese Subaru company.

CHEVROLET NOMAD

Technical Specifications	
Chevrolet Nomad	
Year	2004
Engine	2199cc in-line four-cylinder
Power	250bhp @ 6,200rpm
Torque	325 lb.ft @ 4,200rpm
0-62 mph	Not Quoted
Top Speed	Not Quoted
ENGINE	
Transmission	5 speed Automatic
Drive	Rear wheel drive
DIMENSIONS	
Length	3949mm
Width	1699mm

The Chevrolet Nomad was unveiled by GM at the Detroit Motor Show in 2004. It's neither a saloon, nor an estate, nor an SUV nor any other category of vehicle. Instead it's somewhere in between, recognisable as a Chevrolet, but not like any Chevvy that's yet made it into production.

The Chevrolet Nomad is based on GM's Kappa architecture, which also serves as the foundation for the Pontiac Solstice production model and Saturn Curve concept. Though this is essentially a sports car platform, the Nomad is more functional than a conventional two seater. It's rear-wheel drive, boasting independent front and rear suspensions attached to a rigid chassis that uses a pair of full-length hydroformed frame rails as its foundation. To make space for rear-seat passengers in its 2+2 configuration, the Nomad rides on a longer wheelbase than other Kappa architecture-based concepts.

A turbocharged Ecotec 2.2-liter four-cylinder engine powers the Nomad, which also features a new Hydra-Matic 5L40-E electronically controlled five-speed automatic transmission with finger-operated tap shifting.

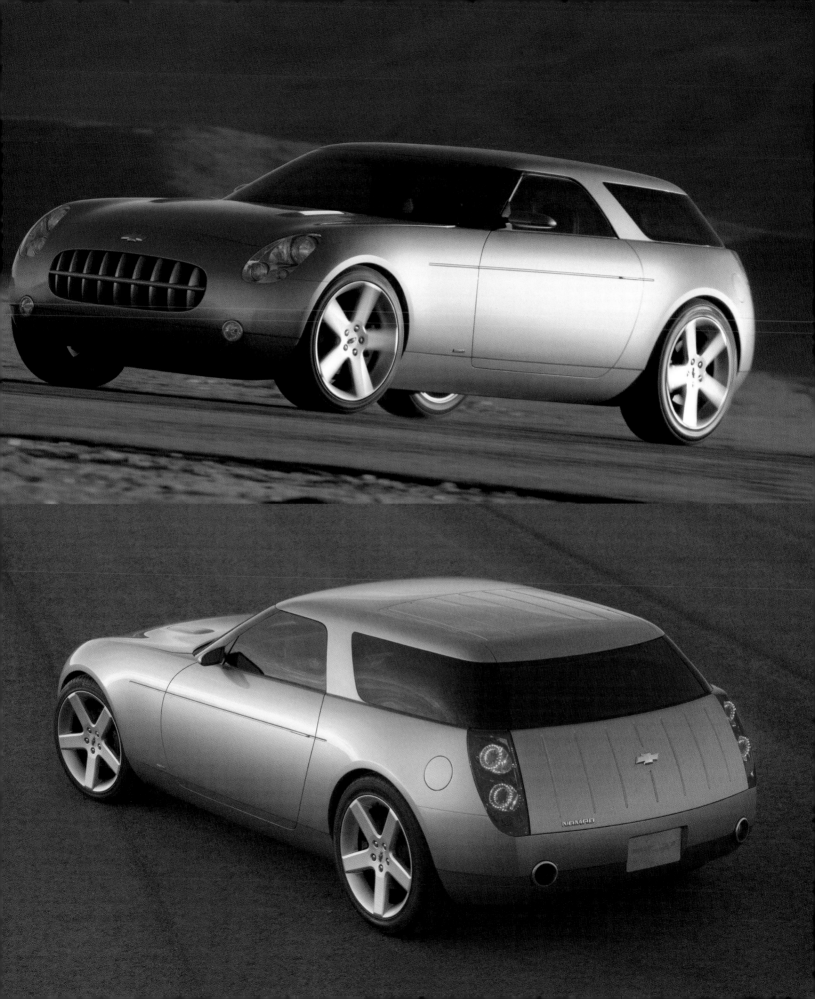

CHRYSLER FIREPOWER

Technical Specifications	
Chrysler Firepower	
Year	2005
Engine	6,100cc V8
Power	Not quoted
Torque	Not quoted
0-62 mph	4.5 sec
Top Speed	175 mph (282 km/h)
ENGINE	
Transmission	5 speed Automatic
Drive	Rear wheel drive
DIMENSIONS	
Length	4383mm
Width	1859mm

Based on the Dodge Viper chassis, the Chrysler Firepower concept, which was first unveiled at the Detroit Auto Show of 2005, is an out-and-out grand tourer. It combines elegance, passion and high performance in a package that falls somewhere between the production Crossfire and the previous year's extreme ME Four-Twelve prototype.

The exterior of the Chrysler Firepower is covered in Hydro Silver Pearl, with dark carbon fibre and polished aluminum accents. But this is more than a show car that looks good on an auto show stand. Computational Fluid Dynamics modeling was used to shape the body with aerodynamics in mind to ensure that Firepower is a viable design despite the car's enormous performance potential. In the same way, this modeling has ensured it's been designed for proper engine cooling as well as appropriate levels of down force in the rear.

Firepower's SRT-developed engine is a 6.1-litre HEMI and although power and torque figures are not disclosed, Chrysler estimates 0-62mph (0-100 km/h) acceleration in 4.5 seconds and a top speed of some 175 mph (282 km/h). A five-speed Autostick transmission offers both luxury and sport driving modes, while suspension and brakes are high-performance units as might be expected on a thoroughbred performance model.

CHRYSLER ME FOUR-TWELVE

Technical Specifications

Chrysler ME Four-Twelve

Year	2004
Engine	6,000cc V12
Power	850bhp @5,750 rpm
Torque	850 lb.ft. @ 2,500 rpm
0-62 mph	2.9 sec
Top Speed	248 mph (400 km/h)
ENGINE	
Transmission	7 speed Automatic
Drive	Rear wheel drive
DIMENSIONS	
Length	4541mm
Width	1998mm

Chrysler's spectacular quad-turbo V12-powered mid-engined ME Four-Twelve is probably the most advanced Chrysler car ever built. Planned to be the ultimate engineering and design statement, the concept was actually developed in just one year from start to finish. In this respect it also reveals Chrysler Group's immense capabilities.

The heart of the ME Four-Twelve is its all-aluminum, quad-turbo, 6.0-litre V-12 engine. With electronic sequential multipoint fuel injection and a 9.0:1 compression ratio, the ME Four-Twelve's AMG-developed engine delivers 850 bhp @ 5750 rpm, with 850 lb. ft. of torque. The specific power output translates to 142 bhp/litre, and with a curb weight of just 2880 lbs. (1310 kg), the ME Four-Twelve has the weight-to-power ratio of 3.4 lbs/bhp – each of these sets new performance records and new benchmarks in the super car category.

And, befitting a machine that will play comfortably in the super car league, the performance of the ME Four-Twelve is stunning. In Chrysler's projections and modeling, the ME Four-Twelve goes from 0-60 mph in 2.9 seconds, 0-100 mph in 6.2 seconds and has an estimated top speed of 248 mph (400 km/h). To provide this performance a 7-speed Ricardo Double Clutch Transmission was developed specifically for this vehicle and features the latest double wet-clutch technology and electronic control strategy.

CITROEN C-AIRDREAM

Technical Specifications	
Citroen C-Airdream	
Year	2002
Engine	2,946cc V6
Power	210 bhp @ 6,000 rpm
Torque	260 Nm @ 2,000 rpm
0-62 mph	6.5 sec
Top Speed	241 km/h (150 mph)
ENGINE	
Transmission	5-speed Sequential
Drive	Rear-wheel drive
DIMENSIONS	
Length	Not Quoted
Width	Not Quoted

The Citroen C-Airdream is a study in aerodynamics. This 2+2 coupé with its slender proportions, long wheelbase, long front overhang and short rear overhang, suggests high performance, class and elegance.

The profile of the Citroen C-Airdream coupé shows receding lines converging towards the rear. According to its designers, its waistline which curves towards the rear suggests stability and good roadholding.

Continuing the taut lines of the bonnet the steeply raked windscreen joins the smooth curves of the roof which is fully glazed to provide maximum light for the cabin and optimum visibility for the driver. The concept features drive-by-wire technology, so pedals and gear lever are replaced by steering-wheel mounted controls. Suspension is a further development of Citroen's Hydractive 3 system.

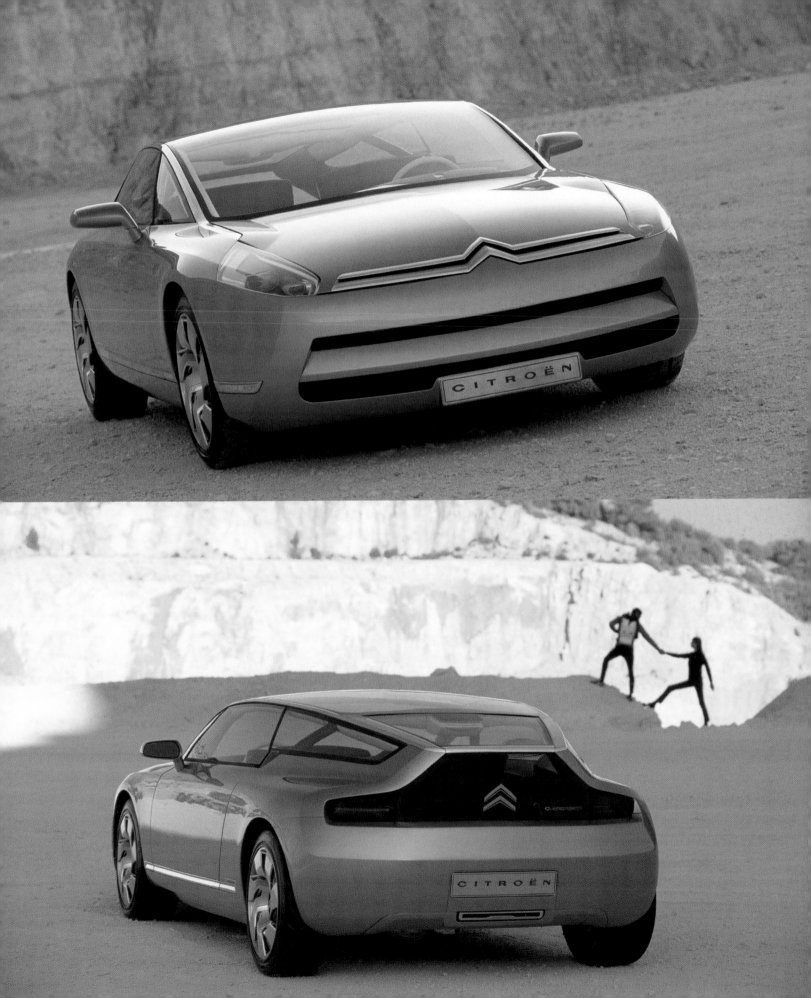

Technical Specifications	
Citroen C-Crosser	
Year	2002
Engine	1,997cc in-line 4-cylinder
Power	90 bhp @ 4,000 rpm
Torque	151 lb.ft @ 1,900 rpm
0-62 mph	Not Quoted
Top Speed	Not Quoted
ENGINE	
Transmission	5-speed Manual
Drive	Four-wheel drive
DIMENSIONS	
Length	4280mm
Width	4280mm

The Citroen C-Crosser illustrates how a future Citroen SUV might look. It's wider than most European vehicles, which allows three-abreast seating and the seating position is well forward to maximize interior space.

The Citroen C-Crosser has a modular body so it can be converted to a pick-up with ease. The tailgate and roof are stowed in the floor at the touch of a button and the rear seats are then concealed revealing a completely flat luggage space measuring 1.9 metres by 1.2 metres. An electric window built into the back of the front seats can be raised to isolate the passenger compartment from the luggage area.

The seating is higher than normal to provide a panoramic view of the road and visibility is further enhanced thanks to the glass roof which forms a continuous line with the windscreen. By-wire technology allows the driver to sit on the right, left or even the middle seat.

Technical Specifications	
DaimlerChrysler ESX3	
Year	2000
Engine	1,500 cc in-line 4-cyl + electric motor
Power	74 bhp
Torque	Not Quoted
0-62 mph	Not Quoted
Top Speed	Not Quoted
ENGINE	
Transmission	Not Quoted
Drive	Front-wheel drive
DIMENSIONS	
Length	4902mm
Width	1880mm

The DaimlerChrysler ESX3 follows two previous ESX concepts, the Dodge Intrepid ESX of 1996 and the ESX2 of 1998. All three are studies in developing a family car with minimum fuel consumption, exhaust emissions and running costs.

This latest ESX study has a hybrid electric powertrain that mates an efficient diesel engine with an electric motor, a lithium-ion battery pack and an electro-mechanical automatic transmission. It also features a lightweight body manufactured from aluminium and injection-moulded thermoplastics with the end result that fuel consumption is an impressive 72 mpg.

Inside the ESX, further weight saving measures are evident. The seats have tubular aluminium frames and aluminium cushion pans while the instrument panel is constructed from expanded polypropylene. A liquid crystal display replaces the conventional instrument pack. Door panels are again lightweight, containing significant amounts of fibre recycled from consumer and industrial waste.

DODGE CALIBER

Technical Specifications	
Dodge Caliber	
Year	2005
Engine	Not quoted
Power	Not quoted
Torque	Not quoted
0-62 mph	Not quoted
Top Speed	Not quoted
ENGINE	
Transmission	Not quoted
Drive	Not quoted
DIMENSIONS	
Length	4414mm
Width	1743mm

Unveiled at the 2005 Geneva Motor Show, the Dodge Caliber is perhaps more than a simple concept car – it also hints at the future direction Dodge is taking for a forthcoming C-segment vehicle. It's has a sporty coupé-style profile yet it promises the stance and space and functionality of an SUV.

The concept Dodge Caliber is finished in a stunning Sunburst Orange paint job but even without that it would attract attention thanks to its sheer surface styling and unmistakeable Dodge DNA. A signature crosshair grille gives the Caliber the distinct face of Dodge. Moving back, there a wide sculpted wheels arches over large 19-inch wheels and tyres. Broad shoulders and a bulging hood hint at power and performance.

A black graphic appliqué runs the length of the roof and melds into an integrated spoiler, creating a coupé-like side view. The forward sweep of the tailgate suggests sporty performance while the rear view is as distinctive as the grille, with its chrome exhaust pipe and large, modular crystal tail lights filling the rear quarters and providing distinct focal points of Caliber's design.

DODGE POWERBOX

Technical Specifications

Dodge Powerbox

Year	2001
Engine 2,700cc in-line 6-cylinder + electric motor	
Power	250bhp
Torque	Not quoted
0-62 mph	7.0 sec.
Top Speed	120 mph (193 km/h)
ENGINE	
Transmission	4 speed Automatic
Drive	Four wheel drive
DIMENSIONS	
Length	5003mm
Width	1956mm

The Dodge Powerbox is an SUV that looks brawny but actually is about as environmentally friendly as it's possible to be. Thanks to hybrid power, with a six-cylinder engine running on Compressed Natural Gas (CNG) combined with an electric motor to boost power when required, its emissions are 60% lower than a comparable SUV.

The combination of petrol engine and electric power provides the performance of a V8 engine but with near-zero emissions. Compared with a conventional Dodge Durango, the PowerBox is projected to achieve 25 mpg resulting in a 60 percent increase in fuel economy without sacrificing horsepower. More astounding than the fuel economy might be how this big vehicle moves off the line: 0-60 in about 7 seconds. That's performance you would expect on a sports car not an SUV.

The Dodge Powerbox still looks the part, however, despite its environmental credentials. It's a rugged sport-utility with enormous street presence and massive capabilities too, thanks to its permanent all-wheel drive transmission system. It's also a practical machine, offering plenty of interior space and a hatchback design that make loading luggage simple and straightforward.

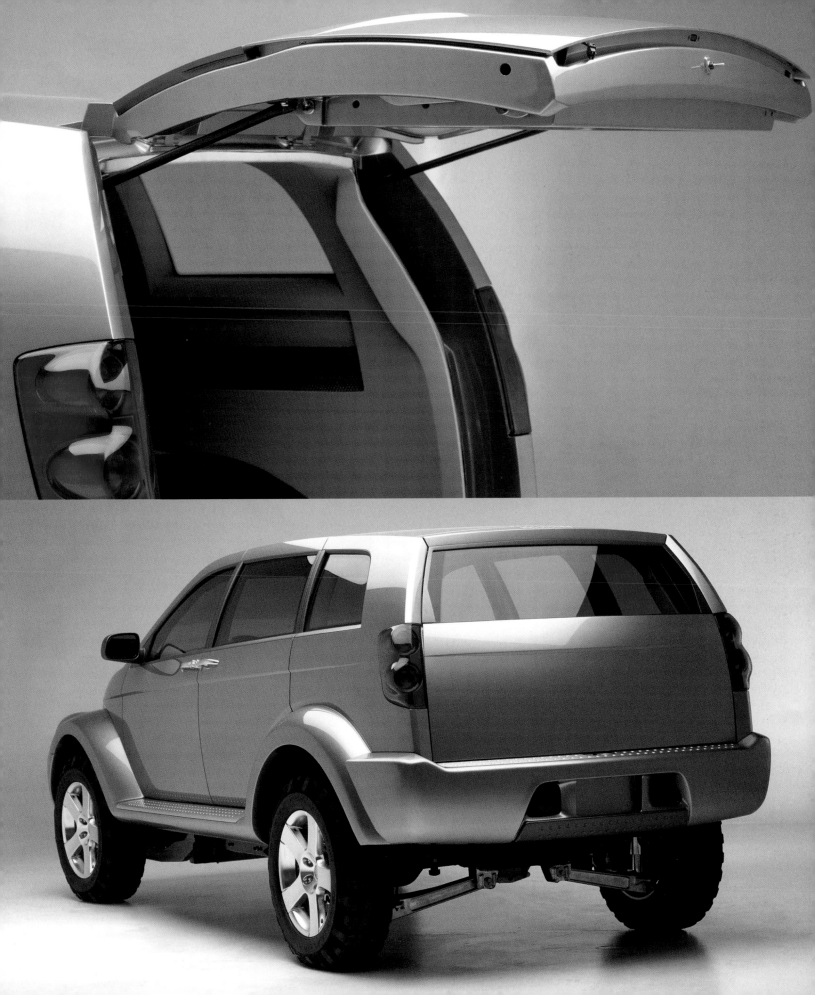

DODGE RAZOR

Technical Specifications	
Dodge Razor	
Year	2002
Engine	2,399cc in-line four-cylinder
Power	250bhp
Torque	230 ft.lb
0-62 mph	6.0 sec.
Top Speed	140 mph (225 km/h)
ENGINE	
Transmission	6 speed Manual
Drive	Rear wheel drive
DIMENSIONS	
Length	3759mm
Width	1752mm

The Dodge Razor is a classic compact sports car, offering two seats, plenty of performance and sharp handling. It's also a simple machine, dedicated to driving pleasure rather than to creature comforts, so the style is minimalist and the interior is devoid of frills and fripperies.

Under the long bonnet of the Dodge Razor concept is a 2.4-litre in-line engine producing a healthy 250bhp which is more than enough to offer 140mph performance and acceleration from 0-62mpg in just six seconds. The purpose of the Razor goes further however: it's also intended to provide pure and unadulterated driving pleasure.

For this reason the interior offers the necessities for driving and no more. No power windows or mirrors, no radio or leather power seats. Instead it offers its two occupants lightweight, competition-style seats, four-point racing harnesses, a little storage behind the seats and the pure joy of driving. Even the appearance of the interior reflects this search for basic simplicity – it's finished in body colour and extruded aluminium. Similarly the exterior lacks any ornamentation except for the chrome bumpers, a racing-style aluminium fuel filler cap and classic door handles and mirrors.

DODGE SUPER8 HEMI

Technical Specifications	
Dodge Super 8 HEMI	
Year	2001
Engine	5,785cc V8
Power	353bhp
Torque	395 ft.lb
0-62 mph	5.7 sec.
Top Speed	155 mph (250 km/h)
ENGINE	
Transmission	4 speed Automatic
Drive	Rear wheel drive
DIMENSIONS	
Length	4724mm
Width	1879mm

Under the bonnet sits the real story of this concept car with its roots in the 1940's and 1950's: the famous HEMI engine that made its name on the NASCAR racetracks. The latest version is a 5.7-litre V8 with hemispherical combustion chambers and two spark plugs per cylinder that produces a healthy 353bhp.

Though the Super 8 HEMI's engine harks back to earlier years, its specification is absolutely up to the minute. Futuristic gadgets include a 6.4 inch screen incorporated into the fascia and two 8.4 inch touch screens for the rear seat passengers. Infotronic speech recognition and Text-to-Speech telematics technology maintains a real-time link with cyber space. There is also an internet-based off-board navigation system with e-mail access.

If that weren't enough, the Super 8 HEMI also features a Home Connection System which allows home appliances such as security systems to be activated or disabled. It also allows the driver to activate entertainment systems from the car through an internet-based remote interface. For good measure, rear seat passengers can enjoy an entertainment system which includes location-based trivia games which can be played with other passengers, or with a player in another car by way of GPS location technology.

FIAT TREPIUNO

Technical Specifications	
Fiat Trepiuno	
Year	2004
Engine	Not Quoted
Power	Not Quoted
Torque	Not Quoted
0-62 mph	Not Quoted
Top Speed	Not Quoted
ENGINE	
Transmission	Not Quoted
Drive	Front-wheel drive
DIMENSIONS	
Length	3800mm
Width	1305mm

The Fiat Trepiuno, first revealed at the 2004 Geneva Motor Show, is Fiat's modern day take on the famous 500 model, the car that started Italy's love with motoring more than 50 years ago. Although few details of this concept have been disclosed, it's known that Fiat intends to put a similar model into production.

The intimate connection between the Fiat Trepiuno and the Fiat 500 is clear from the form and the shape of this concept. But there are other similarities too, not least that the Trepiuno is a genuinely small car at just 3.3 metres in length. Despite this, there is plenty of cabin space for up to four adults thanks to the concept's long wheelbase and clever interior design.

The seats, for example, are made from layers of polyurethane to create a flexible, comfortable structure that absorbs loads while taking up an absolute minimum of space. And the fascia in front of the front passenger can be deflated to allow more leg room when necessary. The Fiat 500 was an icon of its time, and when put into production it's likely that the Fiat Trepiuno will be too.

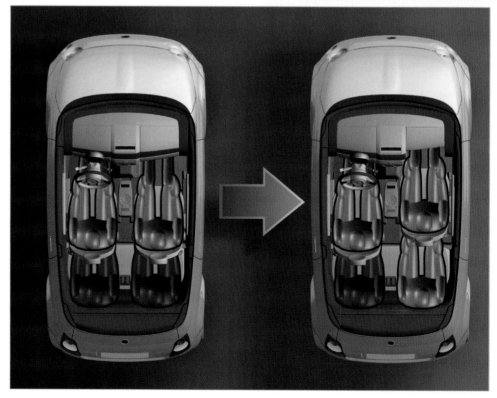

FIAT FORMULA4

Technical Specifications	
Fiat Formula4	
Year	1996
Engine	1,998 cc in-line 5-cylinder
Power	147bhp @ 6,100 rpm
Torque	138 lb.ft @ 4,500 rpm
0-62 mph	8.5 sec
Top Speed	Not Quoted
ENGINE	
Transmission	5-speed Manual
Drive	Front-wheel drive
DIMENSIONS	
Length	4155mm
Width	1820mm

The Fiat Formula4, created by ItalDesign on a Fiat Brava platform is a four-seat roadster, intended to provide wind-in-the-hair fun motoring without the normal sports car restriction of just two seats in the front.

Power for the Fiat Formula4 comes from a five-cylinder Fiat Brava DOHC 2-litre engine with four valves per cylinder. The platform is also borrowed from the Brava but there the similarities end. While the Brava is a sensible and practical car, the Fiat Formula4 is designed for younger people wanting a cheap basic model which can be customized to suit their individual tastes.

This example, first unveiled at the 1996 Geneva Motor Show, has a lightweight body constructed from carbon fibre. But ItalDesign claimed that it would be equally as feasible to build a similar body at substantially lower costs, from the same sort of resin materials used in the manufacture of surf boards.

FORD 021C

Technical Specifications	
Ford 021C	
Year	1999
Engine	1,596cc in-line four cylinder
Power	101bhp @ 6,000rpm
Torque	196 lb.ft. @ 4,000rpm
0-62 mph	Not quoted
Top Speed	Not quoted
ENGINE	
Transmission	4 speed Automatic
Drive	Front wheel drive
DIMENSIONS	
Length	3601mm
Width	1648mm

Ford's 021C urban concept vehicle was first unveiled at the Tokyo Motor Show in 1999. The intention of designer Marc Newson was to create a car that would appeal to drivers aged 21 and younger – consumers who are brand literate, extremely technologically aware and want quality products which express their individuality.

According to Ford's head of design J Mays the whole approach to the 021C was different. While car designers normally approach everything from an automotive perspective, the 021C treats the car as a cultural icon: "We have created a distinct point of view with this car and if you don't get it, don't worry – you're probably not meant to", he said.

The car, which was constructed at Ford's Ghia design studio in Turin, is built round Ford's small car platform and is a three box saloon with extremely short overhangs. Although it has a wheelbase 37mm longer than the production Ford Ka, the 021C is actually 19mm shorter overall. Its carbon fibre exterior features simple shapes and clean surfaces with little decoration – the door handls, for example, are simple aluminium buttons.

Technical Specifications	
Ford Forty-Nine	
Year	2001
Engine	3,900cc V8
Power	Not quoted
Torque	Not quoted
0-62 mph	Not quoted
Top Speed	Not quoted
ENGINE	
Transmission	5 speed Automatic
Drive	Rear wheel drive
DIMENSIONS	
Length	Not quoted
Width	Not quoted

Just after the second world war, Ford's '49 model with its radical slab sides and integrated body and fenders served as a symbol of optimism for the future. 50 years on the Ford Forty-Nine concept car offers a trip down memory lane as it harks back to America's cruising and custom car craze.

To create the concept Forty-Nine Ford's designers went back to the car's roots – simple shapes, clean body panels and modern conveniences. It's smooth appearance is achieved by an all-glass upper body structure with totally concealed pillars and windscreen wipers. The interior is also a modern interpretation of the original car's simple design. It has a cantilevered bench-style front seat though a floating centre console which runs the length of the interior gives the impression of four-passenger bucket seating while also serving to stiffen the vehicle's structure.

The concept is powered by a 4.0-litre V8 from the Ford Thunderbird and the engine bay itself is finished in satin black, stainless and chrome metal finishes throughout. This under-hood design is yet another homage to the hot-rodders' obsession with both performance and appearance.

FORD FAB1

Technical Specifications	
Ford Thunderbird FAB 1	
Year	2004
Engine	Classified, no details released
Power	Classified, no details released
Torque	Classified, no details released
0-62 mph	3.0 sec (est.)
Top Speed	250+ mph (402+ km/h)
ENGINE	
Transmission	Automatic
Drive	Front wheel drive
DIMENSIONS	
Length	7010mm
Width	1828mm

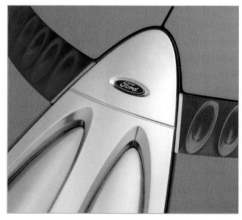

Not exactly a concept car, more a flight of fancy, the Ford Thunderbird FAB 1 was created for the Thunderbirds film as personal transport for Lady Penelope. Available in any colour as long as it's pink, the FAB 1 is larger than life with massive power and presence.

Ford Design Europe created FAB 1 as a fantastical version of the Thunderbird. It's got six wheels, a bubble canopy and it transforms into a jet plane or a hydrofoil at the touch of a button. From the outside, there's a touch of the production Thunderbird about the front end, but there the similarity ends. Inside FAB 1's cockpit features classic elements, with old dials and switches mixed in with a more contemporary luxury design aesthetic.

Interestingly the twin front wheels had to be designed so that one turns more than the other, otherwise it counteracts the first one. If this had not been done, FAB 1 would not have been able to travel round corners.

Ford Focus Vignale	
Year	2004
Engine	Not quoted
Power	Not quoted
Torque	Not quoted
0-62 mph	Not quoted
Top Speed	Not quoted
ENGINE	
Transmission	Not quoted
Drive	Front wheel drive
DIMENSIONS	
Length	Not quoted
Width	Not quoted

The Ford Focus Vignale is two cars in one – a stylish and sporty coupé when the weather is poor and a sleek convertible when the sun shines. Then, at the touch of a button, the boot tilts open and the retractable hardtop folds into the boot area. Though billed as a design study, observers at the Paris Show where the Focus Vignale was revealed suspect a production version may follow soon.

What is unusual about the Ford Focus Vignale concept is the sheer quality of its craftsmanship and the premium materials that have been specified for its interior. There is also more than a hint of the classic Italian sports car about this vehicle. The clean lines of the exterior are highlighted by the use of polished aluminium which evokes the chrome of past Italian touring cars. There is also a narrow polished aluminium strip that runs the length of the car at its sills, mirrored by another horizontal strip at the lower edge of the side windows.

The concept's glass is uniquely coloured in Acqua, a blue-green tint that changes the personality of the car when it is in coupé mode. Also unique to the Focus Vignale are special highly sculpted 20-inch alloy wheels which combine polished aluminium outer surfaces with machined aluminium on the visible inner surfaces.

FORD GT90

Technical Specifications	
Ford GT90	
Year	1995
Engine	5,933 cc V12
Power	720 bhp @ 6,300 rpm
Torque	660 lb.ft @ 4,750 rpm
0-62 mph	3.1 sec
Top Speed	383 km/h (238 mph)
ENGINE	
Transmission	5-speed Manual
Drive	Rear-wheel drive
DIMENSIONS	
Length	4470mm
Width	1963mm

The Ford GT90 was more than yet another supercar concept. It was also Ford's way of bringing its new 'Edge' design to a wider audience. The Ford GT90 looked like a Stealth Bomber with its triangular flat surfaces intersecting with one another.

Originally intended for a limited production run, the Ford GT90 took its inspiration from the legendary GT40 of the 1960's. Both are low-mid-engined two-seaters with amazing performance, but not even the Le Mans winning GT40 could have matched the potential of the Ford GT90's incredible 720 bhp V12 engine with its four turbochargers.

The chassis of the GT90 derives from racecar design. It features a honeycomb aluminium chassis with a carbon fibre body and a ceramic exhaust system that derived from space shuttle technology. In the end the GT400 never made it into production but nevertheless this unique one-off had a material effect on future Ford design.

Ford Indigo

Technical Specifications	
Ford Indigo	
Year	1996
Engine	5,935 cc V12
Power	435 bhp @ 6,100 rpm
Torque	405 lb.ft @ 5,250 rpm
0-62 mph	3.9 sec
Top Speed	274 km/h (170 mph)
ENGINE	
Transmission	6-speed Sequential
Drive	Rear-wheel drive
DIMENSIONS	
Length	4470mm
Width	1963mm

Two examples of the Ford Indigo were built – one was a non-drivable show car and the other was a fully functional prototype. It had a race-derived chassis and a newly-designed V12 engine that later powered the Aston Martin DB7 Vantage and Vanquish.

Reynard Racing designed the chassis of the Ford Indigo which consists of a carbon fibre and aluminium honeycomb composite tub. This monocoque structure is light and immensely strong and it has the front suspension and running gear attached directly to it. The rear suspension is located directly on the transaxle while the engine is bolted to the rear bulkhead of the chassis and acts as a load-bearing member – which is typical racecar practice.

The V12 engine is based on Ford's 3.0-litre Duratec V6 and it shares the same bore, stroke, pistons, rods, valves and other components. It also shares the Duratec's high torque characteristics and relatively low fuel consumption. The engine was developed in just 18 months from conception to first dynomometer test.

FORD SHELBY GR1

Technical Specifications

Ford Shelby GR-1

Year	2004
Engine	6,300cc V10
Power	605bhp @ 6,750rpm
Torque	501 lb.ft. @ 5,550rpm
0-62 mph	4.0 sec
Top Speed	200+ mph (322+ km/h)
ENGINE	
Transmission	6 speed Sequential
Drive	Rear wheel drive
DIMENSIONS	
Length	4413mm
Width	1834mm

Ford's Shelby GR-1 is the latest in a long line of high performance concept cars that the company has produced. This time it sports a 605bhp V10 engine and a stunning polished aluminium body that combines scultptured surfaces and a sleek fastback muscular design.

The Shelby GR-1 is no mere show car. It's a fully engineered, production-feasible roadgoing, driveable project vehicle. At its heart is a modified version of the aluminium chassis used on the rear-engined Ford GT but in this case the V10 engine originally created for the Ford Shelby Cobra project in 2003, is mounted at the front.

Butterfly doors are employed on the Shelby GR-1 concept and these feature distinctive teardrop side glass graphics that create an elongated appearance and which blend seamlessly into integrated door-release handles. Inside the car a race-inspired interior has seats with carbon shells and fixed backs. The seats incorporate removable Alcantara inserts

that are individually tailored to the occupants body shape and size.

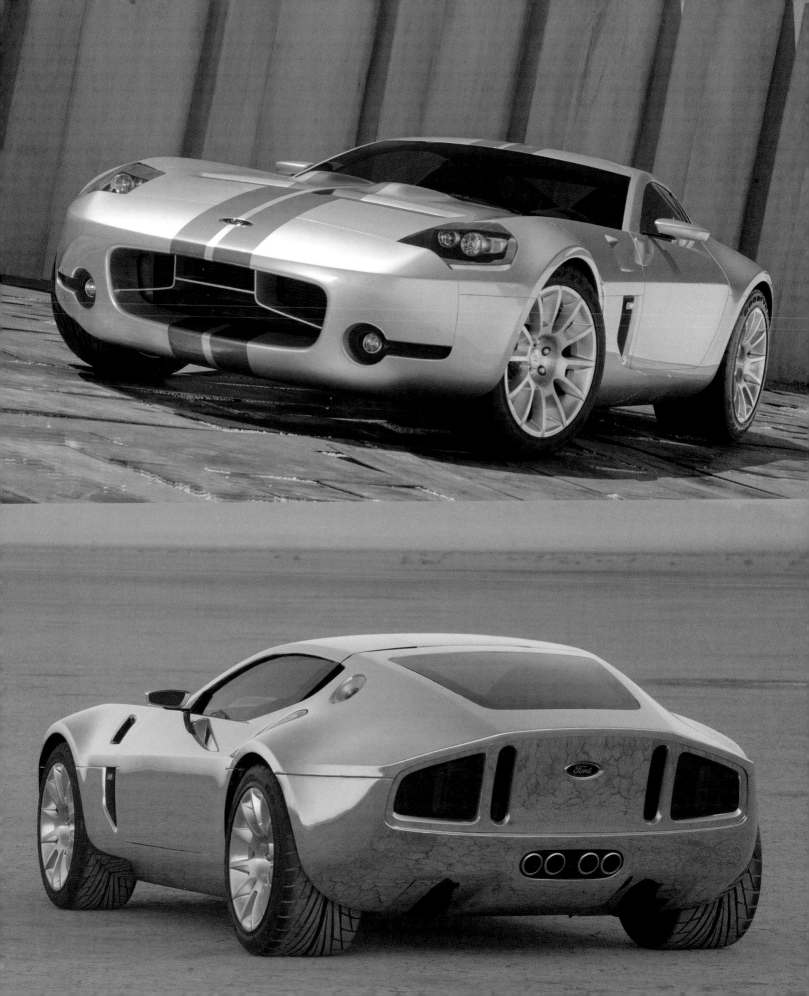

GMC GRAPHYTE

Technical Specifications	
GMC Graphyte	
Year	2005
Engine	5,300cc V8 and electric motor
Power	300 bhp
Torque	325 lb.ft
0-62 mph	Not Quoted
Top Speed	Not Quoted
ENGINE	
Transmission	5-speed Automatic
Drive	Four-wheel drive
DIMENSIONS	
Length	4767mm
Width	2004mm

The GMC Graphyte concept vehicle is a refined SUV with all the performance and capability expected of an all-wheel drive truck, but with the added advantage of fuel consumption some 25% less than normal, thanks to the latest hybrid engine technology.

The GMC Graphyte uses a two-mode full hybrid system that uses mainly electric propulsion at lower speeds and around town while a second mode is employed at higher speeds or when full power is required for climbing steep hills. A 300 volt NiMH battery pack sits under the rear seats and this drives two compact electric motors when required. A series of gears that provide an infinite range of drive ratios is contained within the case of a conventional Hydra-Matic automatic transmission.

In terms of design the GMC Graphyte not only provides hints of a future direction for GMC trucks. It also shows how aerodynamic performance can be radically improved on vehicles of this size and nature.

GM Hy-Wire

Technical Specifications	
GM Hy-Wire	
Year	2002
Engine	Fuel cell with electric motor
Power	60 kW
Torque	159 lb.ft
0-62 mph	Not Quoted
Top Speed	160 km/h (100mph) (Est.)
ENGINE	
Transmission	8.67:1 ratio planetary gear
Drive	Front-wheel drive
DIMENSIONS	
Length	4357mm
Width	1670mm

GM'S Hy-Wire concept, first shown at the 2002 Detroit Motor Show, was developed in the next eight months before the Paris Motor Show to be the world's first driveable vehicle that combined a hydrogen fuel cell with by-wire technology.

The Hy-Wire's propulsion and control systems are all contained in an 11-inch thick skateboard chassis which maximizes the interior space for five passengers and their luggage. There is no engine to see over, no pedals to operate, just a single unit called X-Drive which controls steering, braking and other systems electronically, that can be easily set for either right or left-hand drive.

Power comes from fuel cells which use hydrogen which is stored in pressurised on-board tanks to create DC electric power which is then converted to alternating current to drive the electric motor. No batteries are required even at peak loads. As a result of this and other concepts, GM expects to have a significant number of fuel cell cars on the market by 2010

GM SEQUEL

Technical Specifications	
GM Sequel	
Year	2005
Engine	fuel cell and battery electric motors
Power	60 kW
Torque	1740 lb.ft at the wheels
0-62 mph	Under 10 secs
Top Speed	145 km/h (90mph)
ENGINE	
Transmission	10.95:1 ratio planetary gear
Drive	Four-wheel drive
DIMENSIONS	
Length	4994mm
Width	1966mm

GM's Sequel combines future technologies – fuel cell power – with a modern and production-feasible crossover body design. In this instance the intention all along was to show the technology in a realistic vehicle rather than in an outlandish dream machine.

The Sequel's designers studied global design trends when searching for influences, both inside and outside the concept vehicle. These included trends in shapes, colours, lighting and materials as seen in a wide range of products from Scandinavian furniture to the latest Asian-designed cell-phones and sports shoes.

Contemporary colours inside the Sequel include plum, rice and wasabi, along with metal and wood accents. Also incorporated in the interior is a new gel material for the armrests and load-floor strips – a translucent silicone rubber that permits backlighting through the material to provide a comforting ambient glow to the interior of the car. This lighting theme is continued in LED-lit trenches in the instrument panel.

GMC Terracross

Technical Specifications	
GMC Terracross	
Year	2001
Engine	3,400cc V6
Power	185bhp
Torque	205 lb.ft
0-62 mph	Not Quoted
Top Speed	Not Quoted
ENGINE	
Transmission	4-speed Automatic
Drive	Four-wheel drive
DIMENSIONS	
Length	4368mm
Width	1905mm

The GMC Terracross is not just another SUV – it's also a pick-up truck and a five-seat convertible, all in a single flexible package. It's designed to appeal to young urban professionals wanting functionality, innovation and capability.

The GMC Terracross gains its flexibility thanks to an ingenious three-part glass roof, a reconfigurable mid-gate and gliding rear doors. The panels can be opened almost the whole length of the roof or when moved forward they create an open cargo box at the rear of the vehicle. A mid-gate, with a retractable rear window is integrated into the second seat row backrest and this can be flipped forward and stowed flush with the seat to crerate an extended flat cargo floor.

The concept also employs a unique hinge system that allows the rear doors to glide rearward parallel to the sides of the vehicle. Combined with standard front doors and no B-pillar, this offers unrivalled access.

HUMMER H3T

Technical Specifications

Hummer H3T

Year	2004
Engine	3,460cc in-line 5-cylinder
Power	350bhp @ 6,000rpm
Torque	350 lb.ft @ 3,600 rpm
0-62 mph	Not Quoted
Top Speed	Not Quoted
ENGINE	
Transmission	4-speed Automatic
Drive	Four-wheel drive
DIMENSIONS	
Length	4443mm
Width	**1893mm**

The H3T proves that not all Hummer vehicles have to be huge in size. This is a mid-sized truck concept first revealed at the 2004 Los Angeles Show, and it's a glimpse of the future of the brand, when the range will include smaller, non-SUV configured vehicles.

Like all Hummers the H3T is designed to offer awesome off-road performance and although it's smaller than production Hummers it still retains the classic Hummer proportions – wide stance, low roofline and wheels at the corners.

The tyres on this concept were created by GM and Nike Design and built by BF Goodrich to offer maximum traction in all environments. Nike also influenced the interior, with the use of its Sphere material on the H3T's seats. This lightweight material, used by Nike for sports clothing, can cool or warm the body as required. The seats also have Nike Epic backpacks which are integrated into the seat back clamshells and released with elastic bungees.

ItalDesign Corvette Moray

Technical Specifications	
ItalDesign Corvette Moray	
Year	2003
Engine	6000cc V8
Power	400bhp @ 6,500rpm
Torque	Not Quoted
0-62 mph	Not Quoted
Top Speed	Not Quoted
ENGINE	
Transmission	4 speed Automatic
Drive	Rear wheel drive
DIMENSIONS	
Length	4540mm
Width	1950mm

One of the stars of the 2003 Geneva Motor Show, the ItalDesign Corvette Moray was intended to be both a tribute to an iconic brand and a celebration of 50 years of Chevrolet Corvette production because, along with the Ford Mustang, the Corvette is the supreme symbol of the great US sports car.

The starting point of ItalDesign's Corvette Moray was the chassis and mechanicals of a production Chevrolet Corvette. The running gear was then clothed in a new body whose design was intended to resemble a Moray Eel – long and slender with rippling sinuous lines. At the front is the unmistakeable Corvette grille, but there's a far more curved bonnet that is contrasted by an upright, sharply cut-off tail.

The doors are an interesting design, being hinged in the middle so the semi-dome units merge the side windows into the roof. When the doors are swung open, according to ItalDesign they offer a reminder of a seagull's wings. In the words of Fabrizio Giugiaro of ItalDesign, "With the Moray we vowed to honour the rhetorical principles of the American muscle car". While the Moray may have pleased an American audience, in Europe at the Geneva Show, it received a less than rapturous greeting.

ITALDESIGN MACHIMOTO

Technical Specifications

ItalDesign Machimoto	
Year	1986
Engine	1781cc in-line four-cylinder
Power	139bhp @ 6,100rpm
Torque	124 lb.ft @ 4,250rpm
0-62 mph	Not Quoted
Top Speed	Not Quoted
ENGINE	
Transmission	5 speed Manual
Drive	Front wheel drive
DIMENSIONS	
Length	3985mm
Width	1680mm

ItalDesign's radical Machimoto was neither a car nor a motorcycle. Designed by Giorgio Giugiaro and his son Fabrizio, it's a hybrid design that is one of the most original and eccentric ever to come out of ItalDesign. Fabrizio said it combined the merits of a car with those of a motorcycle while Giorgio wondered if they had not instead merely focused on the defects of both.

The Machimoto is powered by a Volkswagen Golf 16V engine, and it also has four wheels, seat belts and a large anti-roll bar, but that doesn't make it a car. Driver and passengers sit on two rows of saddle seats, and – like on a motorcycle – there's no protection from the elements. What is impressive is that the Machimoto seats six on comfort and eight at a pinch, and all in an overall length of under four metres.

According to Giorgio Giugiaro, part of Machimoto's purpose was to recapture the style of the Dune Buggy, the beach version of the VW Beetle that had virtually been outlawed by stricter safety and environmental protection laws. He believed there could still be a niche for this sort of vehicle and that an open leisure car should be a viable option. In addition, he noted that Machimoto was more friendly than a traditional buggy that seated only two.

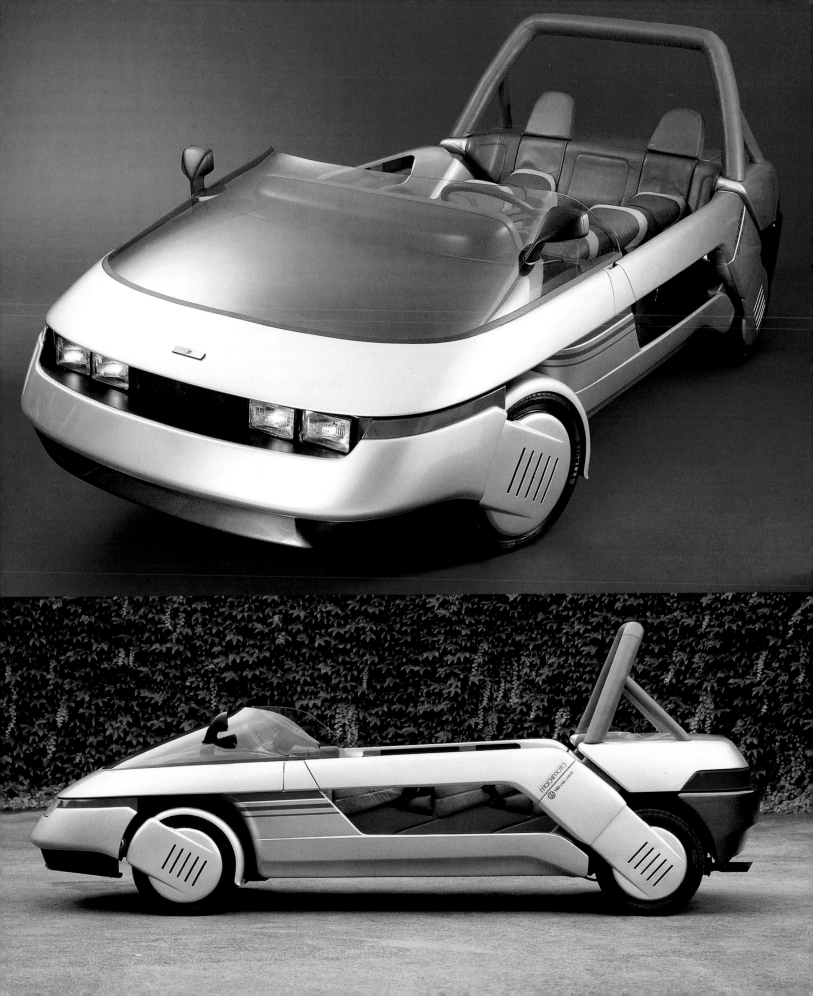

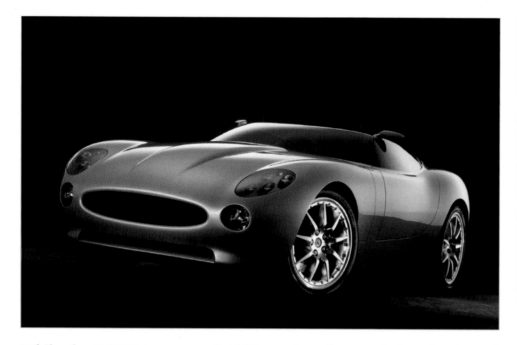

Technical Specifications	
Jaguar F-Type	
Year	2000
Engine	3,000 cc V6
Power	240 bhp
Torque	Not Quoted
0-62 mph	Not Quoted
Top Speed	Not Quoted
ENGINE	
Transmission	6-speed Automatic
Drive	Rear-wheel drive
DIMENSIONS	
Length	3772mm
Width	1863mm

While the XK180 concept of 1999 was based around the chassis and mechanicals of a production car – the XK coupe – the F-Type concept, first revealed at the Detroit Show in 2000 had no such restraints so the design team could make it more compact.

When the F-Type concept was first shown there were high expectations that this car would go into production as a worthy successor to the legendary E-Type. And in fact Jaguar did announce the following year that production was planned, but circumstances sadly prevented this.

The concept is distinctively Jaguar in style as well as being contemporary and functional. What its designers succeeded in doing was injecting some of the E-Type's DNA without making this a pastiche of a 1960's sports car. There is nothing retro about the F-Type, either in style or technology. It was designed to take a variety of powertrains, starting with the 240 bhp AJ-V6 engine that had recently been introduced on the S-Type saloon.

Jaguar Kensington

Year	1990
Engine	4896cc V12
Power	295bhp @ 5,500rpm
Torque	Not Quoted
0-62 mph	Not Quoted
Top Speed	Not Quoted
ENGINE	
Transmission	4 speed Automatic
Drive	Rear wheel drive
DIMENSIONS	
Length	4896mm
Width	1770mm

In 1990 ItalDesign unveiled the Jaguar Kensington at the Geneva Motor Show to showcase what a new and smaller Jaguar saloon might look like. It was well-received by most observers but Jaguar executives were less enthusiastic, pointing out that in order to service the V12 engine it would be necessary to take out the front windscreen.

Though Jaguar showed little interest in the Kensington concept, ItalDesign's work was by no means wasted. In 1991 a new production car was revealed at the Tokyo Motor Show and that car – the Lexus GS300 – clearly owned much to the Kensington design. Strangely, according to ItalDesign boss Giorgio Giugiaro the President of Toyota, Edi Toyoda, himself approved the design for Lexus in 1989.

The Kensington was based around the mechanicals of a V12 Series 3 XJ saloon and its lines hark back to many of the themes of the old Mk2 and S-Type Jaguar saloons, in particular the way in which the tapered bonnet rises above the level of the wings, the shape of the rear side windows and the way in which the rear haunches suggest forward movement and agility. Although Jaguar had only just been acquired by Ford at the time the Kensington appeared and so the UK company then had access to funds for new product development, ItalDesign were not commissioned to create a production car. So the Kensington remains simply a testament to the talents of the Turin company.

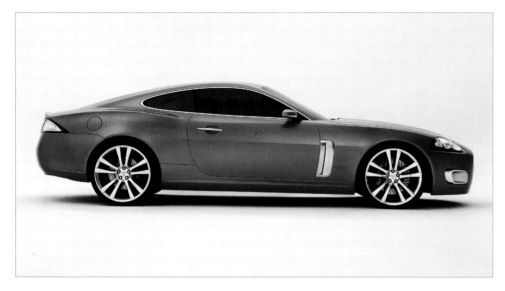

Technical Specifications

Jaguar Advanced Lightweight Coupé	
Year	2005
Engine	4,196cc V8
Power	395bhp @ 6,100rpm
Torque	399 lb.ft @ 3,500rpm
0–62 mph	under 5 sec
Top Speed	180 mph (290 km/h)
ENGINE	
Transmission	5 speed Manual
Drive	Rear wheel drive
DIMENSIONS	
Length	4775mm
Width	1830mm

The Jaguar Advanced Lightweight Coupé represents the very essence of Jaguar, its heart and soul. This concept, first revealed in 2005, shows what direction Jaguar will take in the future, both in terms of its styling and appearance and in terms of its underlying engineering.

Designed by Ian Callum, the Jaguar Advanced Lightweight Coupé is a logical progression from the earlier R-Coupé and R-D6 concepts from Jaguar. It's beautiful in its lines, muscular without going over the top but also relatively practical thanks to its hatchback design. Were it a production car it would also be the most potent 2+2 Jaguar has ever produced, thanks to its lightweight aluminium construction and powerful V8 engine. The concept also promises fabulous handling and response thanks to a sophisticated suspension set-up, impressive low-down torque and numerous dynamic driver aids such as Adaptive Cruise Control and Computer Active Technology Suspension.

Inside, tan leather and aluminium inserts provide a modern but luxurious ambiance. Gearshift paddles are mounted on the steering wheel, the first time this technology has been seen on a Jaguar car.

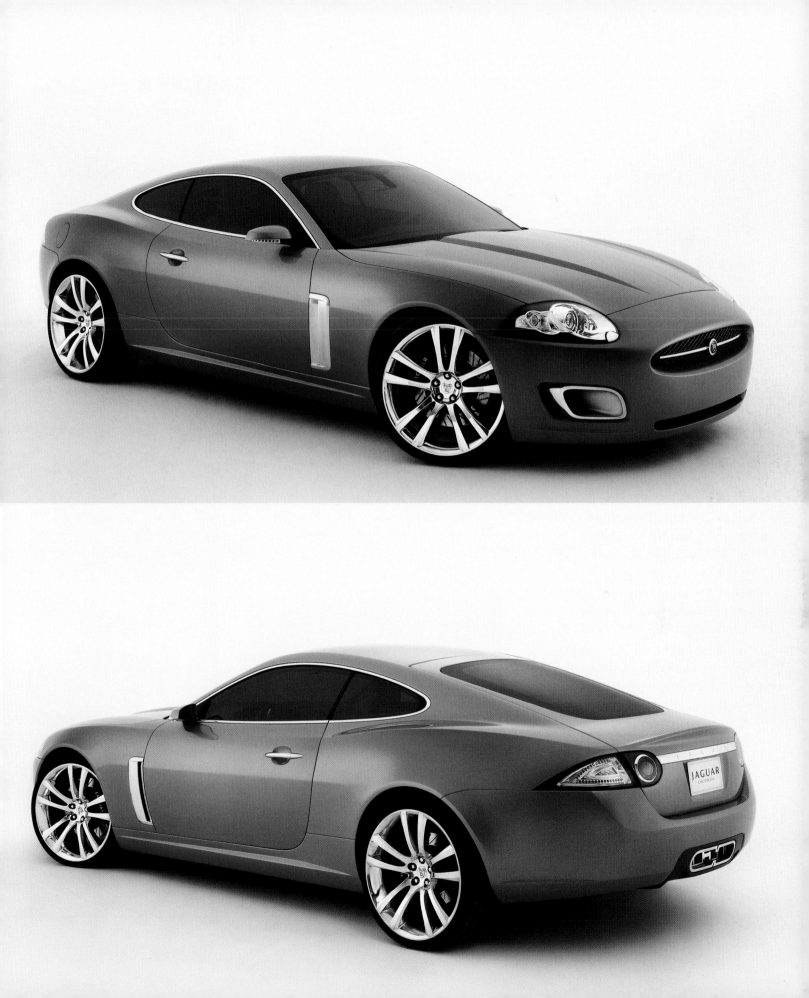

Technical Specifications

Jaguar XK180 Roadster

Year	2000
Engine	3,996cc V8
Power	450bhp @ 6,150rpm
Torque	445 lb.ft @ 3,600rpm
0-62 mph	4.7 sec
Top Speed	180 mph (290 km/h)
ENGINE	
Transmission	5 speed Automatic
Drive	Rear wheel drive
DIMENSIONS	
Length	4417mm
Width	1830mm

The Jaguar XK180 Roadster was unveiled at the 2000 Detroit Show as a follow-up to the XK180 coupé that debuted at the previous year's Paris Show. Built to celebrate the 50th Anniversary of the XK series sports car, the XK180 draws its inspiration from some of the most successful production and race cars in Jaguar's illustrious history.

Just as the XK120 was named after its top speed – 120mph _ so the XK180's name reflects its performance potential. The engine is a supercharged and intercooled variant of the AJ-V8 unit modified to produce 450bhp. The five-speed automatic transmission incorporates a new selector system which allows the driver to change gears using pushbuttons located on the steering wheel.

To create the XK180 Jaguar's Special Vehicle Operations (SVO) group started with a production XKR and shortened the chassis by five inches. Lightweight aluminium body panels formed to a design penned by Keith Helfet from Jaguar's Styling department were then added, while under the bonnet the production V8 engine was modified for added power and torque. Finally 20-inch wheels with ultra-low profile Pirelli PZero tyres and

a Brembo braking system were adopted. The result is a fully operational prototype capable of sustained high performance.

Jeep Commander	
Year	1999
Engine	Electric motors front and rear
Power	Not Quoted
Torque	Not Quoted
0-62 mph	Not Quoted
Top Speed	Not Quoted
ENGINE	
Transmission	Not Quoted
Drive	Four-wheel drive
DIMENSIONS	
Length	4724mm
Width	2032mm

When the Jeep Commander concept was originally conceived the intention was that it should be powered by a fuel-cell drivetrain that used petrol to create electricity to drive the car. The concept revealed at the 1999 Detroit Show was actually a pure battery-drive electric vehicle.

Normal fuel cells convert hydrogen and oxygen into water vapour and electricity to create an ultra-clean power source but since hydrogen is difficult to store, DaimlerChrysler investigated a converter system that would transform petrol into hydrogen and carbon dioxide. At the time, engineers couldn't get the technology to work so the Jeep Commander concept was a straightforward electric vehicle.

One technology that was interesting was the Commander's injection-moulded body panels and an ingenious 'on-demand' luggage rack that sits flush with the roof for improved aerodynamics when not in use but can be raised when needed. The suspension can also be raised or lowered by up to four inches depending on whether the concept is being used on the road or off-road.

JEEP HURRICANE

Technical Specifications	
Jeep Hurricane	
Year	2005
Engine	2 x 5,700cc V8
Power	670bhp
Torque	740 lb.ft.
0-62 mph	5.0 sec
Top Speed	Not quoted
ENGINE	
Transmission	5 speed Automatic
Drive	Four wheel drive
DIMENSIONS	
Length	3856mm
Width	2033mm

The Jeep Hurricane is billed as the most powerful 4x4 ever built, which is not surprising considering it's fitted with not one but two 5.7-litre HEMI V8 engines, one in the front and the other at the back. Between them they churn out a massive 670bhp and 740 lb.ft of torque. Truly this is as close to a go-anywhere machine as ever existed.

Though the Jeep Hurricane is fitted with two engines, the vehicle is actually powered by four, eight, 12 or 16 cylinders depending on the driver's needs. At full power, it is capable of accelerating from 0-60 mph in less than five seconds. Even more astonishing is it's off-road ability because thanks to its 37-inch tyres and near-vertical approach and departure angles there's almost no hill it can't climb. Add to this the Hurricane's turning circle of zero – both front and rear wheels can be turned inwards so the car turns in its own length – it's also the most manoeuvrable 4x4 ever made.

The monocoque body is made from light but ultra-strong carbon fibre and both suspension and powertrain are mounted directly to this body. An aluminimum spine runs under the body which functions as a complete skid plate system.

Technical Specifications	
Jeep Willys	
Year	2001
Engine	1,600 cc in-line 4-cylinder
Power	160 bhp
Torque	155 lb.ft
0-62 mph	10.2 sec
Top Speed	140 km/h (87 mph)
ENGINE	
Transmission	4-speed Automatic
Drive	Four-wheel drive
DIMENSIONS	
Length	3607mm
Width	1778mm

The Jeep Willys is a back-to-basics homage to the legendary Jeep of the second world war, but in a thoroughly modern package involving the use of high-tech composite body materials that are 100% recyclable.

Unveiled at the 20001 Detroit Motor Show, the Jeep Willys features plastic-body technology that allows designers to create shapes that would not be possible with stamped metal construction while maintaining high levels of rigidity. In this instance, a one-piece carbon fibre body is moulded to a lightweight aluminium frame.

Power comes from DaimlerChrysler's 1.6-litre in-line four-cylinder engine that is supercharged for added performance. It is mated to a four-speed automatic transmission that can be changed on the fly between high and low ratios. The custom suspension and supercharged powertrain are engineered to preserve the rugged capabilities that the Jeep brand is renowned for and the design of the Willys is a good example of a concept that embraces the past while looking to the future.

LAMBORGHINI CALA

Technical Specifications	
Lamborghini Cala	
Year	1995
Engine	3,900 cc V10
Power	400bhp @ 7,200 rpm
Torque	232 lb.ft @ 4,500 rpm
0-62 mph	5.0 sec
Top Speed	305 km/h (195 mph)
ENGINE	
Transmission	6-speed Manual
Drive	Rear-wheel drive
DIMENSIONS	
Length	4394mm
Width	1905mm

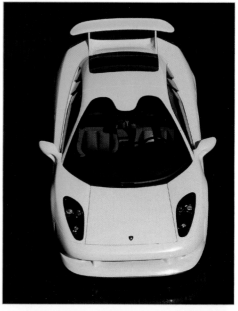

The Lamborghini Cala is a fully operational prototype created by ItalDesign for the 1995 Geneva Motor Show where it was one of the biggest stars of the Show. It was commissioned by Lamborghini as a possible replacement for the Jalpa, but sadly the Cala never made it into production.

When Audi bought Lamborghini in 1998 the German manufacturer immediately halted development of the V10-powered Cala and instead directed all available resources into a V12-powered replacement for the Countach. The Jalpa replacement, which the Cala was intended to be, would not reach the market until 2003 when the Gallardo was launched. Though technically impressive, the Gallardo lacked the style of the Cala.

The Cala was a fully drivable prototype and its performance was as impressive as its appearance: Top speed was over 300 km/h (195 mph) and its acceleration from 0-62 mph was timed at just 5.0 seconds.

LAMBORGHINI CONCEPT S

Technical Specifications	
Lamborghini Concept S	
Year	2005
Engine	4,961 cc V10
Power	500bhp @ 7,800 rpm
Torque	376 lb.ft @ 4,500 rpm
0-62 mph	Not Quoted
Top Speed	Not Quoted
ENGINE	
Transmission	6-speed Manual
Drive	Rear-wheel drive
DIMENSIONS	
Length	Not Quoted
Width	Not Quoted

Lamborghini renewed a great tradition at the 2005 Geneva Motor Show when it unveiled the Concept S. Like the 350 GTS and Miura Roadster that preceded it, the Lamborghini Concept S is a one-off, extreme expression of all that makes the Lamborghini brand special.

Created at the Centro Stile Lamborghini in Bologna, the "Concept S" is an extreme interpretation of an "open car". Using the Gallardo as a basis, the designers drew inspiration from the classic single-seater racing cars of the past to create this design study.

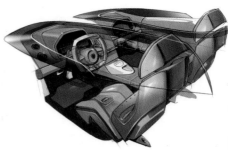

Classic single-seaters did not have a traditional windscreen, but instead used aeroscreens in order to direct air over the head of the driver - and so does the "Concept S". These divide the cabin into two distinct compartments, giving the car an aggressive and futuristic look and also creating a space between them that acts as an additional air inlet for the powerful engine, which is positioned behind the seats. The aerodynamics of the "Concept S" have been optimised thanks to front and rear spoilers and a large rear diffuser.

LANCIA FULVIA

Technical Specifications	
Lancia Fulvia	
Year	2003
Engine	1,747 cc in-line 4-cylinder
Power	140 bhp @ 6,400 rpm
Torque	Not Quoted
0-62 mph	8.6 sec
Top Speed	213 km/h (132 mph)
ENGINE	
Transmission	5-speed Manual
Drive	Front-wheel drive
DIMENSIONS	
Length	4410mm
Width	1810mm

The Lancia Fulvia concept unveiled at the 2003 Frankfurt Motor Show vividly brought back memories of the pretty little Lancia Fulvia coupé built in the 1960's and 1970's. At the time this concept was widely expected to go into production but despite much public acclaim for the new car, it remained just a concept.

Based on Fiat Barchetta chassis and mechanicals the Lancia Fulvia concept's compact size and aluminium body ensured low overall weight. As a result its 1.8-litre in-line engine was potent enough to provide a top speed of 213 km/h (132 mph) and 0-62 mph acceleration in 8.6 seconds.

In design terms, Lancia's stylists based the appearance and dimensions on the old Fulvia Coupé but produced a concept that was thoroughly modern with a truncated tail and extremely dynamic shape that tapers from front to rear. Inside there are two bucket seats and an additional luggage compartment under the parcel shelf. In the concept this space is filled with bespoke bags produced by Trussardi. The cabin is trimmed with leather and aluminium.

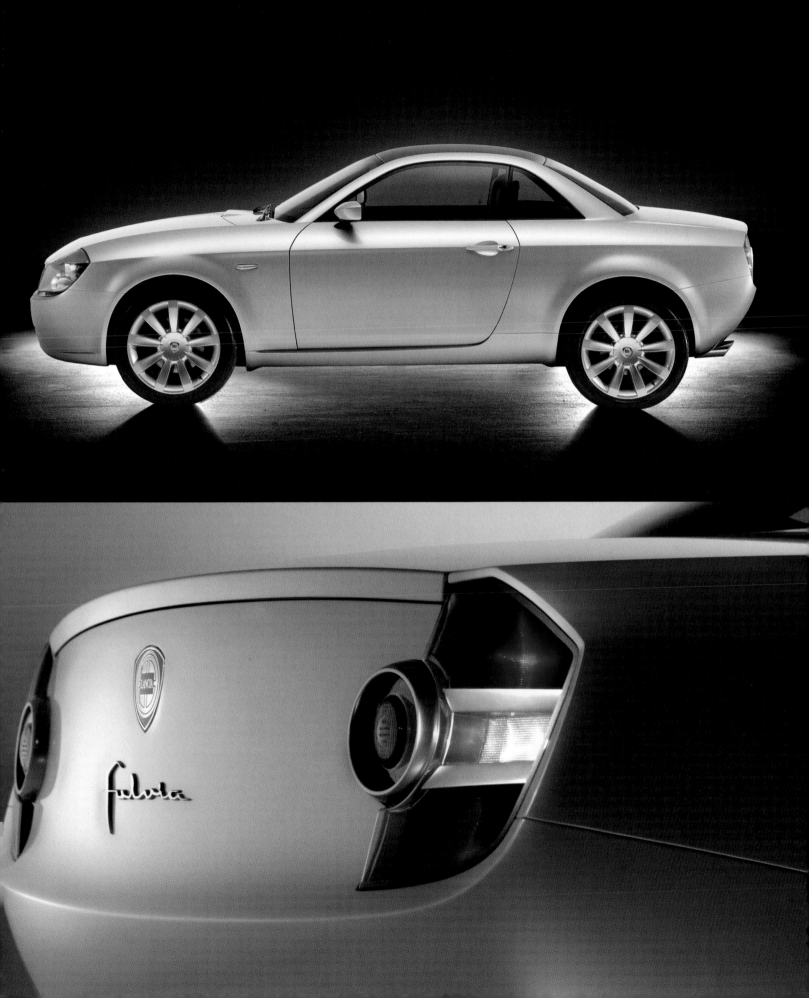

LANCIA MEDUSA

Technical Specifications	
Lancia Medusa	
Year	1980
Engine	1,995 cc in-line 4-cylinder
Power	120 bhp @ 6,000 rpm
Torque	114 lb.ft @ 2,400 rpm
0-62 mph	10.2 sec
Top Speed	140 km/h (87 mph)
ENGINE	
Transmission	5-speed Manual
Drive	Rear-wheel drive
DIMENSIONS	
Length	4410mm
Width	1810mm

The Lancia Medusa was created by Giugiaro's ItalDesign for the 1980 Turin Motor Show as an investigation into the possibilities of designing a four-door practical car that could provide all the driving pleasure of a compact two-seater.

The Lancia Medusa's mechanical layout is that of a mid-ship four-seater in which the engine is placed midships behind the rear seats. This allows a low and very aerodynamic nose and a spacious interior since there is no requirement for a propeller shaft and its tunnel. Further advantages are better weight distribution and the fact that any front-wheel drive engine can be utilized.

It seems like a brilliant example of innovative packaging, but it's one that no major manufacturer has ever taken up, perhaps because of the fact that a rear-mounted engine adversely affects the ride of the car, and controlling noise and heat to the interior becomes a major problem. Giugiaro later utilized some of the Medusa's thinking in the Incas and Asgard concepts.

LAND ROVER STORMER

Technical Specifications	
Land Rover Range Stormer	
Year	2004
Engine	4,197cc V8
Power	390bhp @ 5,750rpm
Torque	406 lb.ft @ 3,500rpm
0-62 mph	7.0 sec (est.)
Top Speed	143 mph (230 km/h)
ENGINE	
Transmission	6 speed Automatic
Drive	Four wheel drive
DIMENSIONS	
Length	4790mm
Width	1930mm

The Land Rover Range Stormer was the company's first ever concept car, a high performance sports tourer SUV which, at the time of its unveiling showcased the future design direction for the company. This concept also previewed the Range Rover Sport model which was launched in 2005.

Though the stunning Range Stormer was always intended to preview a forthcoming production model, certain aspects – such as the two-part doors that hinge upwards to allow access – were clearly not feasible for a road car. But underneath the showy aspects of this concept were some serious themes including a new sportier look which nevertheless retained the classic Land Rover design language – in the clamshell bonnet, 'floating' roof, straight waistline and short front overhang. Though a very modern interpretation this is obviously a Land Rover.

In technological terms the Range Stormer also hinted at what was to come in production models, particularly a new and unique platform, height-adjustable air suspension and Terrain Response, an electronic system allowing the driver the select one of six electronic modes according to ground conditions.

LEXUS LFA

Technical Specifications	
Lexus LFA	
Year	2005
Engine	4,388 cc V8
Power	Not Quoted
Torque	Not Quoted
0-62 mph	8.6 sec
Top Speed	322 km/h (200 mph)
ENGINE	
Transmission	Not Quoted
Drive	Rear-wheel drive
DIMENSIONS	
Length	4399mm
Width	1859mm

The Lexus LFA revealed at the 2005 Detroit Motor Show blends outstanding performance with what is promised as a bold new styling direction for the Lexus brand. Though the LFA is just a concept, it's a realistic vision of how Lexus might address a supercar in the near future.

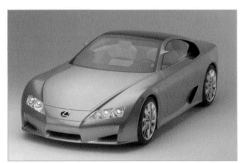

With parent company Toyota heavily involved in Formula 1 motor racing, it was only a matter of time before the company starting thinking about a high-performance road car. Though this concept features a V8 engine, in production any powertrain and drivetrain configuration would most likely be strongly influenced by what is being used in competition – which means a V10 engine.

The styling of the Lexus LFA is simple in both form and function. It is uncluttered, elegant and a statement of understated luxury. The LFA represents a fundamental shift in both style and design for Lexus. It is also an interesting exercise in proportion and packaging because its approach leads to the ultimate weight balance, which is vital to high-speed handling and stability.

LINCOLN L2K

Technical Specifications	
Lincoln L2K	
Year	1995
Engine	3,400 cc V8
Power	250 bhp
Torque	Not Quoted
0-62 mph	Not Quoted
Top Speed	Not Quoted
ENGINE	
Transmission	Not Quoted
Drive	Rear-wheel drive
DIMENSIONS	
Length	Not Quoted
Width	Not Quoted

First revealed in 1995, the Lincoln L2K concept is a compact and pretty two-seat roadster aimed firmly at the market dominated by models such as the Mercedes SLK. Though well received by the public, Ford chose not to proceed to a production version.

The Lincoln L2K has a very short rear-wheel drive chassis but Ford declined to issue any significant details of the car's powertrain. All that is known is that there was a 3.4-litre V8 under the bonnet that produced some 250 bhp.

From the outset, Lincoln-Mercury executives at the Detroit Motor Show where the Lincoln L2K was first unveiled insisted there were no plans to produce this two-seat convertible sport luxury concept. But on the other hand the company would like to be able to offer a small luxury roadster, so this was a good means of testing public reaction. Its name appears to derive from L for Lincoln and 2K for the year 2000, but by the turn of the century the concept had been quietly forgotten in Ford's corridors of power.

Technical Specifications	
Lincoln Mark X	
Year	2004
Engine	3,901 cc V8
Power	280 bhp @ 6,000 rpm
Torque	285 lb.ft @ 4,000 rpm
0-62 mph	Not Quoted
Top Speed	Not Quoted
ENGINE	
Transmission	5-speed Automatic
Drive	Rear-wheel drive
DIMENSIONS	
Length	4701mm
Width	1838mm

The Lincoln Mk X is the company's first convertible featuring a power-folding retractable glass-roofed hard top. This innovative roof is just one aspect of a concept that takes luxury and comfort to new levels – even the boot space is leather lined.

Lincoln has always used the Mark name to denote exceptional products, starting with the Mark 1, the first Continental in 1956. The Mark X is intended to demonstrate the potential of the Lincoln brand by stretching its DNA to a sophisticated roadster. While purely a concept, the Mark X illustrates one possibility for expanding Lincoln into new luxury niches.

The car is based on the rear-wheel drive Ford Thunderbird architecture and is powered by a 3.9-litre V8 delivering 280 bhp mated to a five-speed automatic transmission. Its visual focal point is a new Lincoln grille made from polished aluminium and featuring a pattern of solid horizontal and vertical chrome trim.

Technical Specifications	
Lincoln Navicross	
Year	2003
Engine	4,201 cc V8
Power	280 bhp @ 6,000 rpm
Torque	285 lb.ft @ 4,000 rpm
0-62 mph	Not Quoted
Top Speed	Not Quoted
ENGINE	
Transmission	5-speed Sequential
Drive	Four-wheel drive
DIMENSIONS	
Length	4740mm
Width	1862mm

Describing the Lincoln Navicross is not easy because it won't fit into traditional vehicle segments. It is not a sport coupe, sport saloon nor a sport utility, yet it could be any one of these. It has the size and shape of a sport saloon combined with a sport wagon with the ground clearance of an SUV.

The Lincoln Navicross is based on a modified Lincoln LS platform and employs a full-time four-wheel drive system with adaptive traction control. Its purpose is to explore what a Lincoln crossover vehicle might look like while at the same time testing consumer reaction to a potentially groundbreaking new luxury market sector.

There is no B-pillar on this concept and the centre-opening doors open 90 degrees to provide a huge opening for passenger entry and exit. In the simple fascia switchgear is kept to a minimum with two large LED screens providing information to the driver when required. An unusual design aspect is the hardwood floor on the Navicross.

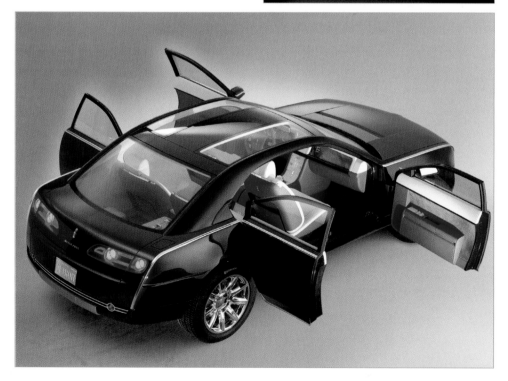

LOTUS ETNA

Technical Specifications	
Lotus Etna	
Year	1984
Engine	3,946 cc V8
Power	247 bhp @ 6,500 rpm
Torque	301 lb.ft @ 5,500 rpm
0-62 mph	4.3 sec. (est.)
Top Speed	291 km/h (180 mph) (est.)
ENGINE	
Transmission	Continuously Variable
Drive	Rear-wheel drive
DIMENSIONS	
Length	4270mm
Width	1840mm

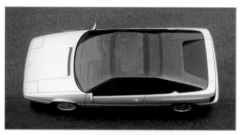

The fabulous Giugiaro-designed Lotus Etna was supposed to bring the British manufacturer up to Ferrari's levels of performance. Unveiled at the Birmingham Motor Show in 1984, it was the undoubted star of the show, and there was much speculation as to how soon it might go into production.

The Lotus Etna was never produced for sale mainly because Lotus could not afford to develop a new V8 engine alone and it failed to attract a wealthy partner. Which is a shame because the Etna could have heralded a whole new era for Lotus. Not only did it display many new technologies, including ABS, active suspension and a computer-controlled Continuously Variable Transmission but it also had a carbon fibre body with an astonishingly low drag coefficient of just 0.90 Cd.

In addition, it had photo-sensitive glass, proximity radar to warn of impending collisions and a central computer controlling the engine management systems – all technologies that were well ahead of their times back in 1984.

MASERATI BIRDCAGE

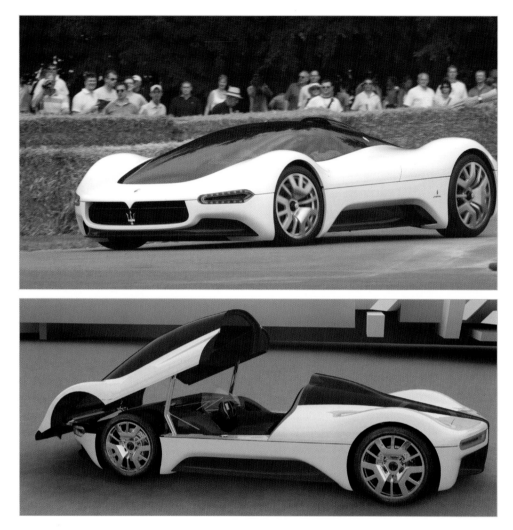

Technical Specifications	
Maserati Birdcage	
Year	2005
Engine	5,998cc V12
Power	700bhp +
Torque	Not quoted
0-62 mph	Not quoted
Top Speed	Not quoted
ENGINE	
Transmission	6 speed Sequential
Drive	Rear wheel drive
DIMENSIONS	
Length	4656mm
Width	2020mm

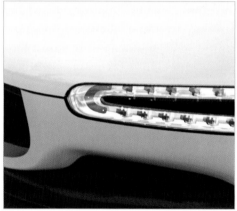

The Maserati Birdcage, a tribute by Pininfarina to the Maserati of the future, impressed many when it was unveiled at the 2005 Geneva Show. Not only did it win the 'Best Concept' award but it also received high praise from Maserati's CEO Karl-Heinz Kalbfell who said "This represents the best interpretation of the Maserati spirit, its heritage and its vision for the future".

The Maserati Birdcage was produced by Pininfarina to celebrate the 75th anniversary of the famous Italian design house. The Birdcage 75th is a concept of a road car where everything – style, performance, use and conception of the car – is extreme so as to achieve the maximum impact. The car is a futuristic extension of the Maserati brand, and at the same time it serves to reinforce the company's potent design heritage.

The Birdcage is based on the Maserati MC12 chassis and is powered by Maserati's V12 engine that produces over 700bhp. Its name is a reminder of the legendary Maserati Tipo 63 – the first 'Birdcage' whose chassis and mechanicals were left on full view under an unusually large windscreen. In the same way, on this modern reincarnation, the carbon fibre nose section is clearly visible through the canopy and the mid-mounted V12 engine is also on view under the rear transparent panel.

Technical Specifications

Maserati Boomerang	
Year	1972
Engine	4,720 cc V8
Power	310 bhp @ 6,000 rpm
Torque	290 lb.ft @ 4,000 rpm
0-62 mph	Not Quoted
Top Speed	274 km/h (170 mph)
ENGINE	
Transmission	5-speed Manual
Drive	Rear-wheel drive
DIMENSIONS	
Length	4340mm
Width	1859mm

The fantastic-looking Maserati Boomerang was first unveiled at the 1971 Turin Motor Show at which time it was a non-functioning model. But by the following year when it was the star of the Geneva Show it had been further developed by ItalDesign and was powered by a Bora-derived V8 engine.

The wedge shape of the Maserati Boomerang was very much an ItalDesign trademark during the 1970's when it could be seen on the Lotus Esprit production car for example. On the Boomerang, the shape was accentuated by the use of large glass panels on the doors and roof to create a greenhouse effect.

Unusually this one-off concept was registered for road use in Germany and remained in private hands for many years before being sold at auction in the 1990's. Since then it has appeared at many of the world's Concours exhibitions, including at the prestigious Pebble Beach event.

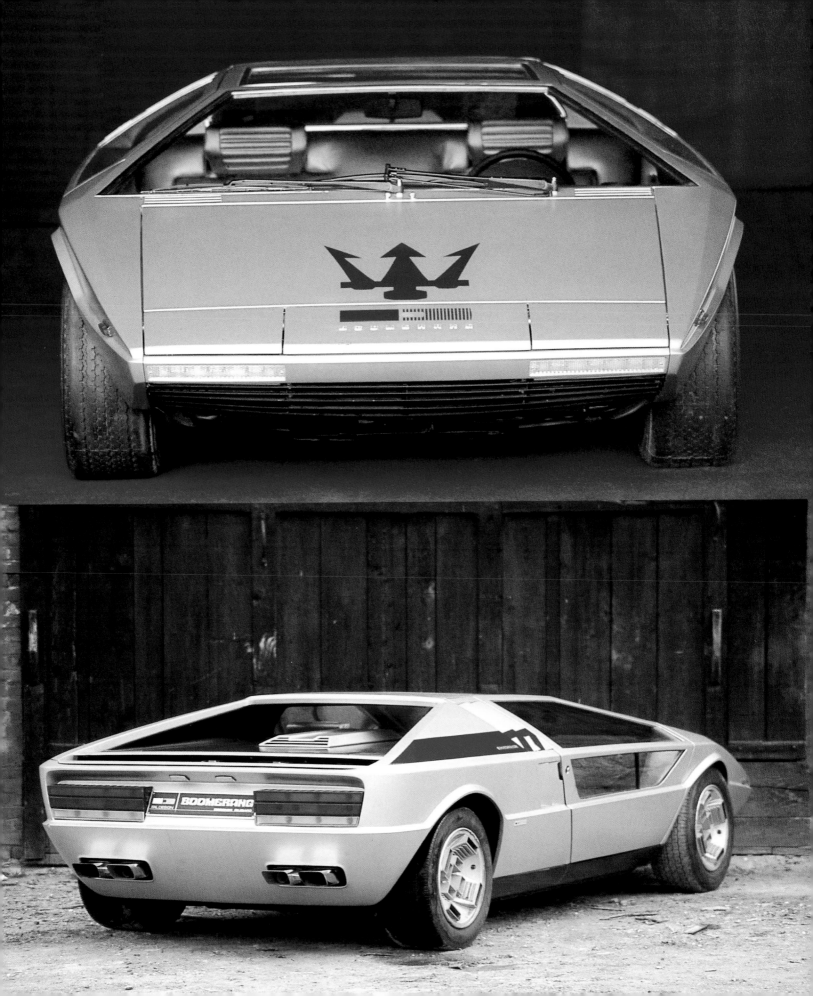

Maserati Buran	
Year	2000
Engine	3,200 cc V8
Power	370 bhp @ 6,250 rpm
Torque	360 lb.ft @ 4,500 rpm
0-62 mph	Not Quoted
Top Speed	Not Quoted
ENGINE	
Transmission	5-speed Sequential
Drive	Four-wheel drive
DIMENSIONS	
Length	4953mm
Width	1956mm

The Maserati Buran is not the prettiest car ever penned by ItalDesign. It was a design exercise aimed at developing a new luxury saloon car for the European and American premium markets. It is large, spacious and provides a multi-purpose interior for work, the family and leisure activities.

The Maserati Buran (the name comes from a cold wind in the Russian Steppes) is the first four-wheel drive Maserati ever built. It is powered by Maserati's 370 bhp twi-turbo V8 coupled to a permanent four wheel drive system via a five-speed sequential automatic transmission.

The large four-door body features sliding rear doors for improved access, a completely flat floor and a moveable centre 'tunnel'. The two-box architecture is based on the design of early 20th century cars, so while other designers were creating long, low aerodynamic shapes, ItalDesign instead opted to a more solid looking unashamedly large and high design that provided optimum interior space. On the concept car the interior is fitted out in suede, wood, leather and chrome.

MAYBACH EXELERO

Technical Specifications

Maybach Exelero

Year	2005
Engine	5,908cc V12
Power	700bhp @ 5,000 rpm
Torque	752 lb.ft. @ 2,500 rpm
0-62 mph	4.4 sec.
Top Speed	218 mph (351 km/h)
ENGINE	
Transmission	5 speed Automatic
Drive	Rear wheel drive
DIMENSIONS	
Length	5890mm
Width	2140mm

The Maybach Exelero was created as a joint venture between Maybach and the tyre company Fulda which wanted an ultra-high performance model on which to test its new high-speed tyres. Since the Maybach Exelero was timed at 218 mph at the Nardo circuit in Southern Italy, it looks like the project was an unqualified success.

The Maybach Exelero is a 700bhp two-seater with a V-12 biturbo engine produced for Fulda as a test vehicle for a newly developed generation of wide tyres. Maybach built this unique model as a modern interpretation of its legendary streamlined sports car from the 1930s which Fulda used for tyre tests at the time of the opening of the Autobahns. Then no-one knew how tyres would cope with the sustained high speeds now possible and back then the plan was to build a car capable of sustaining 124mph (200 km/h).

The Exelero, by contrast, reached far higher speeds in testing. The Exelero, which was built by the prototype specialists at Stola in Turin, is based on the chassis of the Maybach 57 limousine, but because the standard V12 used on the production car would not achieve the desired maximum speed, its capacity was increased from 5.6 to 5.9 litres and a pair of turbochargers were added. Though this project was completed in just 25 months there are no plans for volume production.

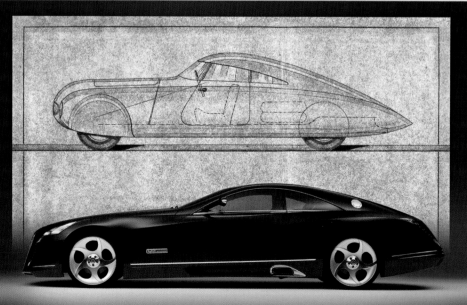

Technical Specifications	
Mazda Ibuki	
Year	2003
Engine	1,599 cc in-line 4-cylinder
Power	180 bhp
Torque	133 lb.ft
0-62 mph	Not Quoted
Top Speed	Not Quoted
ENGINE	
Transmission	6-speed Manual
Drive	Rear-wheel drive
DIMENSIONS	
Length	3640mm
Width	1815mm

The Mazda Ibuki was one of a number of Mazda concepts at the 2003 Tokyo Motor Show, this one clearly signposting the design of the forthcoming Mazda MX5 replacement. The name means 'breathing new life' in Japanese.

The Mazda Ibuki has what is described as a 'super front-midship' layout, similar to that of the roatary-engined RX8 in which all the major mechanical components are located within the wheelbase.

So compared to the production MX5, the Ibuki's 1.6-litre 16-valve four-cyllinder engine and six-speed manual transmission is set some 400mm further back while the air conditioning unit is located behind the seats. The advantage of this layout is that yaw inertia movement is greatly reduced, which improves handling characteristics and improves driver control.

MAZDA MICRO SPORT

Technical Specifications	
Mazda Micro Sport	
Year	2004
Engine	1,966 cc in-line 4-cylinder
Power	148 bhp @ 6,500 rpm
Torque	135 lb.ft @ 4,500 rpm
0-62 mph	Not Quoted
Top Speed	Not Quoted
ENGINE	
Transmission	6-speed Manual
Drive	Rear-wheel drive
DIMENSIONS	
Length	3980mm
Width	1775mm

First revealed at the 2004 Detroit Motor Show the Mazda Micro Sport is a nimble and light five-door concept that was designed specifically for the US market, hence its unveiling in the USA rather than at the Tokyo Motor Show three months earlier.

Despite being a relatively small overall package, the Mazda Micro Sport has an impressively spacious interior – the ability to make more room from less space is a skill Mazda's designers have mastered during years of developing small cars. Headroom is improved by making the A-pillars and side windows more upright than is conventional, and the result is that the compact Micro Sport can still seat four adults in comfort and carry their luggage too.

The luggage compartment is equipped with a detachable partition. When fitted at floor level it allows use of the area beneath the floor as a sub-trunk. Fitted in the upper position the partition can function as a rear shelf and a cover to conceal luggage from view.

MERCEDES BIONIC

The Mercedes Benz Bionic is a concept whose shape is based on a fish. Mercedes designers realized that the tropical Boxfish's shape is almost perfectly aerodynamic, so they set out to replicate the shape in a car.

By taking a lesson from nature and mimicking the shape of the Boxfish, the Mercedes Benz Bionic concept achieves a drag coefficient of just 0.19 Cd – about 65% better than a conventional saloon. The result is fuel consumption figures of up to 84 mpg from the concept's 2-litre four-cylinder diesel engine – a unit that is also extremely clean thanks to new technology that reduces Nitrogen Oxide emissions by 80%.

Those figures are helped by the Bionic's light weight, at just 1,100 kg. This is achieved thanks to a Mercedes innovation called Soft Kill Option (SKO) in which, working with natural principles and computer modeling, material mass and strength is reduced in areas where stress is light on the vehicle and, in some cases, the component is 'killed' altogether.

MERCEDES C112

The Mercedes Benz C112 concept was first revealed at the 1991 Frankfurt Motor Show. Though this mid-engined supercar was never to go into production, its V12 engine appeared in the showroom 600SEL saloon the following year and Mercedes has offered V12 engines ever since.

The biggest surprise of the Mercedes Benz C112 is that it never went into production despite the fact that Mercedes took 700 deposits after the supercar was unveiled in 1991.

The C112 was one of a series of experimental concepts, starting with the C111 in 1969 which was powered by a Wankel rotary engine. A second rotary C111 was produced in 1970 and later the same chassis was used fitted with a turbodiesel engine which broke all the world's diesel performance and acceleration records, reaching 322 km/h (200 mph) in 1978. A twin-turbo V8 version broke yet more records. The C112 was the last of the series.

MERCEDES F100

Technical Specifications	
Mercedes Benz F100	
Year	1991
Engine	2,600 cc in-line 6-cylinder
Power	94 bhp
Torque	Not Quoted
0-62 mph	Not Quoted
Top Speed	Not Quoted
ENGINE	
Transmission	3-speed Automatic
Drive	Front-wheel drive
DIMENSIONS	
Length	Not Quoted
Width	Not Quoted

The Mercedes Benz F100 was one of the company's first forays into the minivan market. This was the first of a series of 'F' concepts – which stands for Forschung, meaning research. It introduced several new safety technologies, including adaptive cruise control.

The Mercedes F100 seated five passengers in a 1-2-2 configuration with the driver sitting in the middle of the car, apparently the safest place. For maximum flexibility all the seats could be removed to increase luggage carrying capacity. The front doors opened outwards then swiveled away for improved access while the sliding rear doors incorporated a section of the roof and lower platform, again to provide the best possible access.

Instead of a rear-view mirror the F100 had two cameras sending images to a monitor on the dashboard. Forward-looking radar warned the driver before changing lanes and detected obstacles, so this was one of the first ever applications of adaptive cruise control technology. Also innovative were solar panels on the roof of the F100 which powered the ventilation system to keep the car cool while it was parked.

Mercedes F300

Technical Specifications	
Mercedes Benz F300	
Year	1997
Engine	1,600 cc in-line 4-cylinder
Power	102 bhp
Torque	Not Quoted
0-62 mph	7.7 sec
Top Speed	211 km/h (131 mph)
ENGINE	
Transmission	5-speed Manual
Drive	Rear-wheel drive
DIMENSIONS	
Length	Not Quoted
Width	Not Quoted

The Mercedes Benz F300 Life Jet combines the feel and cornering dynamics of a motorcycle with the safety and comfort of a car. It has three wheels for stability but like a two-wheeled motorcycle, it leans into bends to increase cornering ability.

The chassis of the Mercedes Benz F300 is made of lightweight aluminium and it is as long as a conventional car but far narrower, to allow leaning into bends. Driver and passenger sit one behind the other, as on a motorcycle, but in more comfort since the F300 has creature comforts such as air conditioning and a stereo system. The roof panels can be removed in good weather and stored in a special compartment behind the rear wheel, thus converting the F300 into an open roadster.

Power comes from the 1.6-litre engine used in the production A-Class car. The engine and electronically shifted transmission are installed between the interior and the rear wheel to save space. Power is transmitted via a toothed belt to the rear wheel.

MERCURY MESSENGER

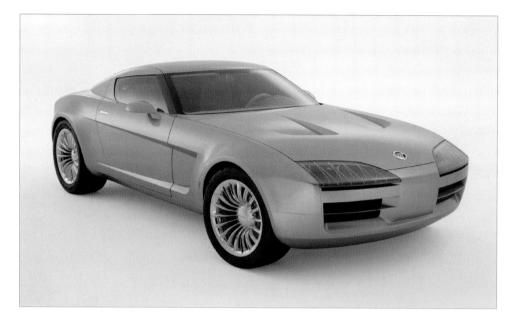

Technical Specifications	
Mercury Messenger	
Year	2003
Engine	4,601 cc V8
Power	Not Quoted
Torque	Not Quoted
0-62 mph	Not Quoted
Top Speed	Not Quoted
ENGINE	
Transmission	6-speed Sequential
Drive	Rear-wheel drive
DIMENSIONS	
Length	4534mm
Width	1938mm

The Mercury Messenger is a high performance, two-seat sports car powered by a V-8 classically driving the rear wheels via a 6-speed sequential automatic gearbox. Its appearance is enhanced by large 20-inch wheels and 305 mm wide tyres at the rear and 19-inch wheels on 275 mm tyres at the front.

The Mercury Messenger has a unique monocoque construction using a composite / aluminum hybrid 'tub' chassis with super-formed aluminium panels bonded to it. The result is a body with high torsional rigidity providing excellent ride and handling properties. Occupant protection is enhanced and noise/vibration/harshness (NVH) is reduced by this method of construction.

The concept is important in that it offers a glipse of the new Mercury DNA and the brand's future design direction. "Messenger is about taut, dynamic surfaces. It's charismatic and modern," said designer Gerry McGovern. "It's about intelligence, connectivity, and it's about distinction. All of these themes will be developed further in Mercury cars and trucks of the near future".

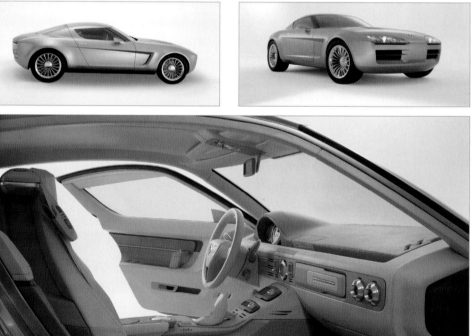

NISSAN QASHQAI

Technical Specifications	
Nissan Qashqai	
Year	2004
Engine	Not Quoted
Power	Not Quoted
Torque	Not Quoted
0-62 mph	Not Quoted
Top Speed	Not Quoted
ENGINE	
Transmission	Not Quoted
Drive	Four-wheel drive
DIMENSIONS	
Length	4310mm
Width	1860mm

The Nissan Qashqai, which is named after a desert-dwelling nomadic tribe living near the Zagros mountains in Southwestern Iran, is described by Nissan as an 'Urban Nomad'. It's a design study for a compact SUV that offers the ruggedness of a 4x4 with the comfort of a traditional car.

Nissan's Qashqai looks like a serious 4x4 and it is equipped with an advanced electronic four-wheel drive system. It's the first concept to come from Nissan's Design Studio in London, whose role is to develop the next generation of Nissans for Europe. No mechanical details of the Qashqai have been revealed.

Rear-hinged back doors open nearly 90-degrees for easy access to its four individual seats thanks to its B-pillarless design. Inside, full-length glazed roof panels give the cabin an airy feeling. An interesting design feature are "invisible" LED headlamps covered in a "clear ink" paint that matches the car's body color, but disappears when light shines through.

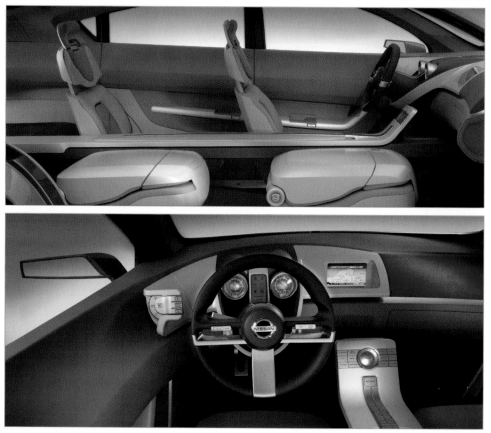

OLDSMOBILE INCAS

Technical Specifications	
Oldsmobile Incas	
Year	1986
Engine	2,260cc V6
Power	230 bhp @ 5,600 rpm
Torque	Not Quoted
0-62 mph	Not Quoted
Top Speed	Not Quoted
ENGINE	
Transmission	4-speed Automatic
Drive	Four-wheel drive
DIMENSIONS	
Length	4445mm
Width	1854mm

The Oldsmobile Incas was another classic Giugiaro design. It's a sleek and stunning four-door saloon with a massive glass area that was based on the platform of the earlier Maya prototype.

It's interesting that the Oldsmobile Incas was produced by ItalDesign at exactly the same time as the company headed by Giorgio Giugiaro was also showing the Machimoto. The two designs could not be more different.

At the heart of the Incas is GM's Quad 4 engine, mid-mounted transversely to allow a four-wheel drive system to be included in the specification. Though this looks like a four-door saloon, in fact the whole of the front section lifts up and hinges forward to allow access to the driver and front seat passenger, while the rear doors are gull-wing designs that swing upwards to allow access to the rear seats.

OLDSMOBILE O4

Technical Specifications	
Oldsmobile O4	
Year	2001
Engine	1,800cc V6
Power	190 bhp
Torque	184 lb.ft
0-62 mph	Not Quoted
Top Speed	Not Quoted
ENGINE	
Transmission	5-speed Manual
Drive	Front-wheel drive
DIMENSIONS	
Length	4115mm
Width	1778mm

The Oldsmobile O4 is not a particularly happy concept as it was the very last glimpse of the future that might have been from the famous American manufacturer. It was unveiled at the 2001 Detroit Show but at the same time it was announced that by GM that the Olds Division was to be closed down.

The Oldsmobile O4 was created as a joint venture between GM's designers and Bertone in Turin. Aimed at younger drivers, it was a front-wheel drive roadster built on an Opel platform and powered by an Opel 1.8-litre Ecotech turbocharged engine.

The O4 was not the most practical of designs in that the two roof panels, made of carbon fibre, had to be snapped off and stored behind the rear seats to provide open-topped motoring. The rear window then could be retracted behind the rear seats too. Inside an 'Info Ring' instrument panel was inspired by Palm Pilot design and involved 10 buttons on the top enge of a display panel that allowed the driver to control all the various functions without the need for conventional switches and gauges.

Technical Specifications	
Opel Eco-Speedster	
Year	2002
Engine	1,251cc in-line 4-cylinder
Power	112bhp @ 4,000rpm
Torque	200 lb.ft @ 1,750 rpm
0-62 mph	4.9 Sec
Top Speed	250 km/h (155 mph)
ENGINE	
Transmission	5-speed Manual
Drive	Rear-wheel drive
DIMENSIONS	
Length	3786mm
Width	1708mm

Is an environmentally-friendly sports car a contradiction in terms? Opel does not think so and its Eco-Speedster, revealed at the 2002 Paris Motor Show proves it is possible to combine genuine high performance with low fuel consumption.

Opel's two-seater prototype is based on the mid-engined Speedster roadster but it features lightweight carbon fibre bodywork and greatly improved aerodynamics. Its drag ratio is an impressively low 0.20 CD, while its weight is a miserly 660kg. Despite being powered by a small 1.3-litre diesel engine, the Eco-Speedster has a top speed of 250 km/h (155 mph) and a test fuel consumption of only 2.5 litres per 100 km. This is thanks in part to newly-developed low-resistance tyres and a special low-friction engine oil.

Occupant comfort is not a priority: the Eco-Speedster features gull-wing doors, a removable steering wheel to assist entry and fixed-back racing seats.

OPEL INSIGNIA

Technical Specifications	
Opel Insignia	
Year	2003
Engine	6,000cc V8
Power	344bhp
Torque	400 lb.ft
0-62 mph	Under 6 Sec
Top Speed	250 km/h (155 mph)
ENGINE	
Transmission	4-speed Automatic
Drive	Rear-wheel drive
DIMENSIONS	
Length	4803mm
Width	1914mm

Star of the Opel stand at both Frankfurt and Tokyo Motor Shows in 2003 was the Insignia concept. Its purpose was to show how Opel's new design language could be translated into a large car for the first time and it revealed, instead of a conservative notchback design, a coupe-style bodyline.

The Opel Insignia has coupe-style bodylines and design details such as the long engine hood with sweeping A-pillars and the inward-tapering front and rear ends. It has short overhangs and balanced proportions and both a strikingly long wheelbase at 2,915mm and wide track at 1,666mm. This allows for a large interior cabin.

The cabin itself offers one significant innovation: he section of the center tunnel that separates the two individual rear seats can be moved back under the boot floor to reveal a folded seat that can be raised electrically to transform the Insignia from a comfortable four-seater for day-to-day business purposes into a sporty five-seat transport vehicle for weekend activities, family and recreation.

PEUGEOT 907

Technical Specifications	
Peugeot 907	
Year	2004
Engine	6,000cc V12
Power	500bhp
Torque	Not quoted
0-62 mph	Not quoted
Top Speed	Not quoted
ENGINE	
Transmission	6 speed Manual
Drive	Rear wheel drive
DIMENSIONS	
Length	4370mm
Width	1880mm

The Peugeot 907 is a concept two-seater coupé, the archetypal touring car that's elegant, comfortable, fast and luxurious. Though the idea harks back to the great coachbuilt coupes of the earlier days of motoring, the 907 is a thoroughly modern and sophisticated twenty-first century machine.

The Peugeot 907 is a sleek and elegant GT sports tourer powered by a massive 6.0-litre V12 engine mounted at the front connected by a propshaft to a rear-mounted six-speed gearbox and transaxle. This provides better weight distribution but also greater cabin space for the driver and passenger.

The structure consists of a carbon fibre shell to which the double wishbone suspension system is attached. The roof and windscreen form a single glazed area while set into the bonnet under a glazed panel are 12 intake trumpets reminiscent of a fairground organ. In the wood and leather trimmed cabin is a digital instrument panel which nevertheless displays information in analogue style while a touch screen on the central console is connected to a PC and provides GPS, MP3 player and other information systems.

PEUGEOT H2O

Technical Specifications	
Peugeot H20	
Year	2002
Engine	Fuel cell electric
Power	Not quoted
Torque	Not quoted
0-62 mph	Not quoted
Top Speed	Not quoted
ENGINE	
Transmission	Direct drive
Drive	Front wheel drive
DIMENSIONS	
Length	4290mm
Width	1689mm

The Peugeot H20, based on the Partner production vehicle, is a futuristic fire engine powered by a highly sophisticated fuel cell battery engine that produces zero emissions. Instead it produces just water and the electricity needed to power the vehicle.

Because the fuel cells produce hydrogen on demand, the Peugeot H20 overcomes the problems associated with conventional hydrogen-powered cars that require the highly volatile hydrogen to be stored under pressure in on-board tanks. Perfect for an urban environment, the H20's only emissions are water.

With its large frontal air intake, feline-shaped lights and plunging bonnet line, this is clearly a Peugeot vehicle, but unlike any production car. Behind the driver and passenger seats is a tank and telescopic ladder, and at the rear where the exhaust would be on a conventional vehicle there are two connections for the water feed or the branch pipe. Naturally the H20 is 'fire engine red', reflected in the interior with its matching metal panels. The cabin itself is designed for two firemen, and features up-to-the-minute communications equipment including GPS, telephone and touch-screen navigation set-up.

Technical Specifications	
Peugeot Hoggar	
Year	2003
Engine	2 x 2,168cc in-line four cylinder
Power	360bhp
Torque	590 lb.ft
0-62 mph	Not quoted
Top Speed	Not quoted
ENGINE	
Transmission	6 speed Manual
Drive	Four wheel drive
DIMENSIONS	
Length	3960mm
Width	1999mm

At first glance the Peugeot Hoggar is an extremely-styled dune buggy. But what that first glance doesn't reveal is that this 2-seater concept is fitted with two transverse engines, one driving the front wheels and the other the rear wheels to create a four-wheel drive vehicle.

Each of the two powertrains consists of a turbocharged four-cylinder Peugeot HDi diesel engine, between them pumping out nearly 360bhp and nearly 500 lb.ft of torque. Each powertrain is controlled by its own electronic unit which distributes inputs from a single accelerator pedal and single gearbox control. If required, the Hoggar can be driven using just one of the powertrains. In this mode, not only does the lightweight Hoggar have a massive range, but thanks to particulate emission filters it's also environmentally friendly.

The central fascia panel features two rev counters while at the top of the central console a vertical touch screen provides speedometer, GPS data and navigation services, on-board MP3 music system and engine warnings.

PEUGEOT QUARK

Technical Specifications	
Peugeot QUARK	
Year	2003
Engine	4 x electric motors
Power	38bhp
Torque	295 lb.ft
0-62 mph	Not quoted
Top Speed	Not quoted
ENGINE	
Transmission	Direct drive
Drive	Four wheel drive
DIMENSIONS	
Length	2380mm
Width	1500mm

The electric Peugeot QUARK was more than just a show car at the Paris Show in 2004. The following month it was transported to Shanghai in China to take part in the annual Bibendum Challenge organised by Michelin to encourage the development of alternative power technology.

The Peugeot QUARK is equipped with a nickel-metal-hydride battery and a fuel cell, which powers not one but four electric motors, one in each of the wheels. With these four motors, the QUARK has four-wheel drive at all times. These direct-drive motors are operated independently from each other by an electronic module, managing the wheel torque based on the way the driver steers, accelerates and brakes. Though the motors do not produce high power outputs, between them they create enormous torque, which provides speedy acceleration particularly from rest.

This electronic module, connected to the four motors, replaces the various mechanical differentials on a standard vehicle and provides more precision and better control. In regenerative braking, the electronic module makes it possible to recover the alternating current generated, transform it into direct current and return it to the battery.

PEUGEOT RC

The Peugeot RC, an elegant sporting 2+2 that was first shown in 2002, is actually not one car but two. The black RC Spades is powered by a petrol engine while the red RC Diamonds has a diesel powerplant. Both share the same basic architecture and styling.

The RC models don't just look good: they also boast some highly sophisticated manufacturing techniques. The structure of the RC is made from carbon pre-impregnated directly onto honeycomb panels, formed and baked in an autoclave. This load bearing shell incorporates a cage roll bar which with the roof creates a highly rigid assembly to which the wings, bonnet and boot and two 'beetle wing' doors are mounted.

The engine and 6-speeed sequential transmission is mid-mounted and drives the rear wheels. Interestingly, both 2.0-litre petrol and 2.2-litre diesel engines produce exactly the same performance on the road, with a top speed of 143 mph (230 km/h) and 0-62mph acceleration in six seconds. The only significant difference is in fuel consumption and carbon dioxide emissions, where the diesel is comfortably superior.

PININFARINA ENJOY

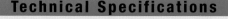

Technical Specifications

Pininfarina Enjoy

Year	2005
Engine	1,795 cc in-line four cylinder
Power	135bhp @ 7,000rpm
Torque	Not quoted
0-62 mph	Not quoted
Top Speed	Not quoted
ENGINE	
Transmission	5 speed Manual
Drive	Rear wheel drive
DIMENSIONS	
Length	3740mm
Width	1790mm

Pininfarina's Enjoy is a sports roadster aimed at younger drivers for whom creature comforts are less important than driving pleasure. It lies firmly in a long Pininfarina tradition of building relatively inexpensive small sports cars which includes the Autobianchi Spider of 1973 and Peugeot 104 Spider of 1974.

The Pininfarina Enjoy is a road car that can also be used on the track. One of its most singular features is that the four wings over the wheels can simply be removed to create an open-wheel car for the racetrack. Also in racing tradition, it has no real windscreen, but instead two small aeroscreens in front of the cockpit. The seats and trim are made from fire and waterproof materials, like a motorbike and in fact the Enjoy is supposed to be used like a motorbike, and so the design includes a compartment in the rear to store helmets, gloves and special overalls produced by Sparco. Two rigid tonneau covers are stored at the front and these can be used to partially close and protect the cabin.

The chassis comes from the Lotus Elise and it is this chassis which is the load bearing structure of the car upon which the body panels are mounted. Power comes from a Lotus four-cylinder engine producing 135 bhp which, given the light weight of the Enjoy vehicle, promises sparkling performance.

PININFARINA OSÉE

Technical Specifications	
Pininfarina Osée	
Year	2001
Engine	2,946cc V6
Power	187 bhp
Torque	196 lb.ft
0-62 mph	Not Quoted
Top Speed	Not Quoted
ENGINE	
Transmission	5-speed Automatic
Drive	Rear-wheel drive
DIMENSIONS	
Length	4150mm
Width	1895mm

The Pininfarina Osée is interesting because it's the first time the famous Italian design house has created a concept car based on Citroen mechanicals. Stylistically it stands out for its massively long wheelbase and virtually zero overhangs.

To allow access to the interior of the Pininfarina Osée, the entire superstructure of the cabin is lifted up by a hydraulic system activated by remote control. Inside three passengers sit in a triangle to make better use of the space. Because this is a pure sports car, the central role of the driving position is emphasized by being right in the middle of the car, with the passengers sitting to the side and slightly behind. The driver's seat is fixed to the car while both the steering wheel and pedals are adjustable to create a comfortable driving position.

The architecture of the Osée, involving a centre-mounted longitudinal engine, is different to any Citroen model before. Also interesting is the central 'spinal cord' effect that runs from the double chevron of the nose of the car right through the cabin to the rear.

PONTIAC PIRANHA

Technical Specifications	
Pontiac Piranha	
Year	2000
Engine	2,200cc in-line four cylinder
Power	212bhp @ 5,900rpm
Torque	203 lb.ft @ 4,600rpm
0-62 mph	Not Quoted
Top Speed	Not Quoted
ENGINE	
Transmission	5-speed Automatic
Drive	Front-wheel drive
DIMENSIONS	
Length	4368mm
Width	1905mm

The Pontiac Piranha was designed to appeal above all to the youth market – a group which not only wants style and performance, but which is also extremely aware of environmental concerns.

Power for the Pontiac Piranha comes from a supercharged version of GM's Ecotec 2.2-litre four-cylinder engine that's been further adapted to create what is claimed to be world-class noise, vibration and harshness (NVH) levels. Aluminium block and cylinder heads reduce weight, increase operating efficiency and improve fuel consumption.

One of the goals of the designers of the concept was to offer a performance car that is both inexpensive to buy and to operate. So the engine is adapted for minimum servicing requirements with the adoption of long-life components and the adoption of an oil life monitoring system that calculates oil life based on engine operation, thus eliminating unnecessary oil changes.

PONTIAC REV

The starting point of the Pontiac Rev, according to its designers, was to take a "rally" sports coupe, and then mix in the versatility to carry friends and cargo. The result is a striking looking, practical, bold and athletic concept with a go-anywhere attitude.

Thanks to permanent four-wheel drive and on-the-fly adjustable suspension the Pontiac Rev promises good traction on all sorts of surfaces. While it's not a full-blown off-roader, its suspension can be raised by two inches when the going gets tough and it's equipped with large, wide tyres for maximum grip.

The Rev's styling is tough, in keeping with its image. Bumpers and rocker panels are made of tough ultra-light carbon fibre composites that extends into the wheel wells and under the bonnet. An interesting feature is the headlights, in which the light sources are placed in a 90-degree angle in the engine compartment. The light beams are reflected outward by mirrors, which respond to steering inputs and thus provide optimal light on the road even in turns.

Technical Specifications	
Pontiac REV	
Year	2001
Engine	3,000cc V6
Power	245bhp
Torque	200 lb.ft
0-62 mph	Not Quoted
Top Speed	Not Quoted
ENGINE	
Transmission	5-speed Sequential Automatic
Drive	Four-wheel drive
DIMENSIONS	
Length	4467mm
Width	1869mm

Technical Specifications	
Renault Koleos	
Year	2003
Engine	1,998cc in-line four-cylinder + electric motor
Power	170bhp @ 6,250 rpm
Torque	271 lb.ft @ 5,400 rpm
0-62 mph	Not quoted
Top Speed	Not quoted
ENGINE	
Transmission	5 speed Manual
Drive	Front wheel drive
DIMENSIONS	
Length	4500mm
Width	1702mm

Unveiled at the 2000 Geneva Motor Show, the Renault Koleos is a cross between a top-of-the-range saloon and a 4x4. Though it is basically a one-box MPV shape, its key characteristic is its variable height suspension system that allows it to tackle rough surfaces when required.

Under the bonnet of the Koleos is a 170bhp 2.0-litre turbocharged petrol engine that drives the front wheels whenever the vehicle is on open roads or motorways. For urban use, however, there is also a 30kW electric motor running on lithium-iron batteries which powers the rear wheels and which produces no emissions. When off-road, the two drive units can be used in tandem providing both additional power and four-wheel drive capability. In this case, any excess power produced by the petrol engine can be used to recharge the batteries.

Inside, four individual seats are constructed from carbon fibre laminates and these are mounted on individual damping cylinders and covered in Connolly leather. The effect is said to be like a horse saddle. Variable height suspension features both pneumatic and hydraulic springs that allow the ride height to be raised up to 100mm. Adjustment is fully automatic and is dependent upon road speed and road surface.

Technical Specifications	
Renault Laguna Roadster	
Year	1990
Engine	1,997cc in-line four-cylinder
Power	210bhp @ 5,500 rpm
Torque	152 lb.ft @ 3,000 rpm
0-62 mph	6.2 sec
Top Speed	155mph (250 km/h)
ENGINE	
Transmission	5 speed Manual
Drive	Front wheel drive
DIMENSIONS	
Length	4114mm
Width	1832mm

The Renault Laguna Roadster concept of 1990 turned out to be the foreshadow of the Renault Spider which went into limited production in 1996. The Laguna Roadster is a modern two-seat sports car with very rounded lines and no windscreen or roof for real wind-in-the-hair motoring – just like the Spider which followed.

The concept's platform is made of four parts: a tubular frame at the front designed to absorb any impacts, a second turbular frame at the rear on which the transverse engine and suspension is mounted, a composite cell made of sheet steel and honeycomb, and a honeycomb partition which acts as a fire bulkhead and adds to the rigidity of the platform.

The Roadster's cabin is set far forward and features just a wind deflector and a tonneau cover for protection from the elements. The tonneau slides aft to allow access for the driver and passenger, while the gullwing doors are semi-automatic and cylinder-activated. The bodywork is made of composite materials, as are the

seats and dashboard. For safety a roll-over bar is raised in one tenth of a second once sensors detect a risk situation.

RENAULT TALISMAN

Technical Specifications	
Renault Talisman	
Year	2001
Engine	4,500cc V8
Power	Not quoted
Torque	Not quoted
0-62 mph	Not quoted
Top Speed	Not quoted
ENGINE	
Transmission	5 speed Automatic
Drive	Rear wheel drive
DIMENSIONS	
Length	4805mm
Width	1950mm

The Renault Talisman is a four-seater top end coupé with a sporty style and a minimalist interior. Under the bonnet is a 4.5-litre 32-valve Nissan engine mated to a 5-speed automatic gearbox. Though no performance figures are quoted, it clearly has the potential to be a superb driver's car.

Talisman has no conventional key for opening the doors. Instead there's a hands-free electronic card to do the job. The concept's long gullwing doors are opened electro-hydraulically to reveal a simple interior with carbon-fibre seats. Though the seats are at a fixed height, each seat cushion is inflatable and so can be adjusted to the perfect height. Since the seats are fixed, it is the dashboard and pedal unit that can be electrically adjusted forwards or backwards to ensure a comfortable driving position.

Talisman's body involves sculptural forms and flowing lines, but it also reveals the fundmental principles of the traditional GT coupé – rounded, muscular and well proportioned. The headlights, which operate on fluid optics technology to reflect light, are fashioned from a strip of glass that extends into the front wings.

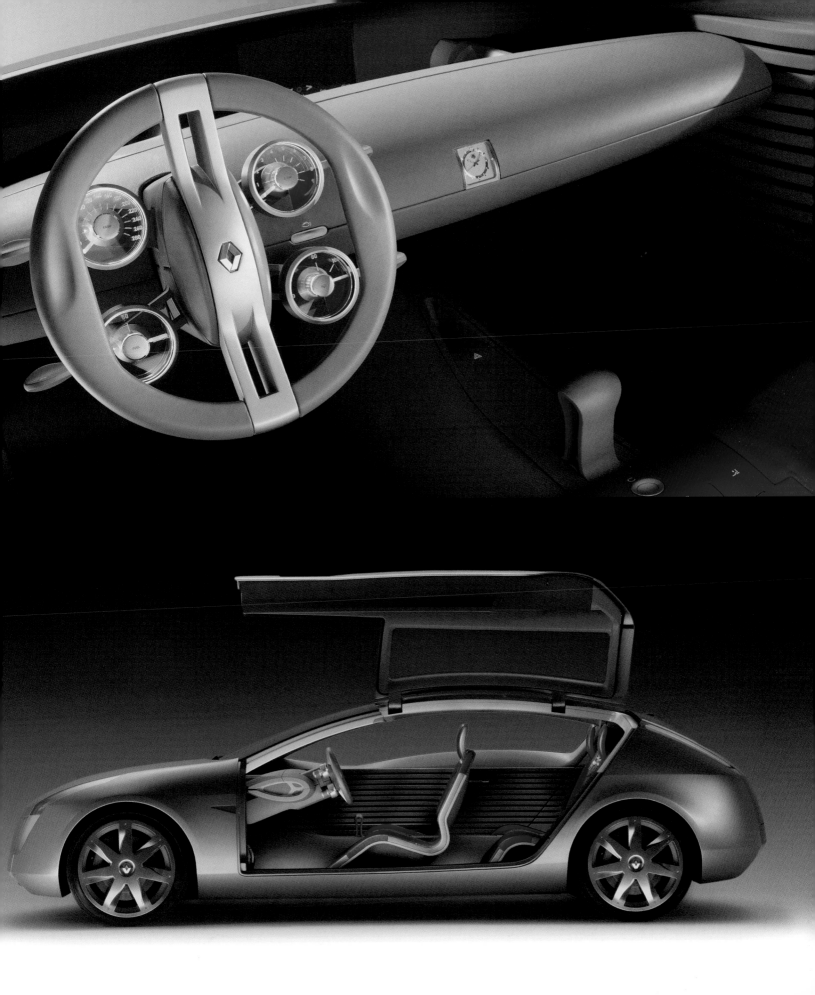

RENAULT ZO

Technical Specifications	
Renault Zo	
Year	1998
Engine	1,999cc in-line four-cylinder
Power	135bhp
Torque	138 lb.ft
0-62 mph	Not quoted
Top Speed	Not quoted
ENGINE	
Transmission	4 speed Automatic
Drive	Rear wheel drive
DIMENSIONS	
Length	3850mm
Width	1850mm

The Renault Zo is a three-seater roadster that's been equipped for off-road work as well when required. First revealed at the 1998 Geneva Show, it featured two major technological developments: an innovative pneumatic suspension system and Renault's new 2.0-litre direct injection petrol engine.

In the carbon fibre-bodied Renault Zo the driver sits in the centre of the car with two passengers slightly further back on either side. Like the Renault Spider there's no windscreen, just an aeroscreen to provide minimal protection from the wind. Beetle-wing doors swing upwards to allow access to the cabin

Where the Zo is new is in its suspension design based on pneumatic springs which make it possible to raise the ride height and alter the stiffness. So on road, a low ride height and stiff suspension setting would be chosen, while off-road, raised ride height and softer springing would be selected. Incidentally the special Michelin tyres fitted to the Zo are more sculpted on the outer side than on the inner side to provide better off-road grip.

ROLLS-ROYCE 100EX

Technical Specifications

Rolls-Royce EX100

Year	2004
Engine	9,001cc V16
Power	Not quoted
Torque	Not quoted
0-62 mph	Not quoted
Top Speed	Not quoted
ENGINE	
Transmission	6 speed Automatic
Drive	Rear wheel drive
DIMENSIONS	
Length	5669mm
Width	1990mm

The 100EX was the first Experimental Car to be produced by Rolls-Royce Motor Cars since BMW Group took over the company in 1998. Based on a lightweight aluminium space-frame, this open-top, four-seat, two-door drophead was designed and produced to celebrate the 100-year anniversary of Rolls-Royce, which fell in May 2004.

There is no plan to produce the 100EX as a series model, said Rolls-Royce at the time though at some stage a convertible version of the Phantom model seems inevitable. While the design of the 100EX and the choice of its special construction materials resonate strongly with Rolls-Royce tradition, both its aesthetic qualities and its technological content place it squarely in the 21st century. A strong nautical theme runs throughout, with bleached teak decking featuring both inside and outside the car. The overall impression, according to RR designer Marek Djordjevic is intended to be that of an elegant motor yacht at speed.

100EX is powered by a 9-litre V16, 64-valve engine. Natural aspiration was chosen over turbo or supercharging to give instant, perfectly smooth pick-up. Drive is delivered through a six-speed automatic gearbox.

TOYOTA VOLTA

Technical Specifications	
Toyota Volta	
Year	2004
Engine	3,300cc V6 plus 2 electric motors
Power	408bhp combined
Torque	Not quoted
0-62 mph	4.0 sec
Top Speed	155 mph (250 km/h)
ENGINE	
Transmission	Direct drive
Drive	Four wheel drive
DIMENSIONS	
Length	4358mm
Width	1925mm

The Toyota Volta, created by ItalDesign, is based on Toyota's hybrid power system as used on the Lexus RX400. Under the bonnet is a 3.3-litre V6 petrol engine while a separate electric motor powers the front and rear wheels, creating an all-wheel drive system that provides both high performance and low emissions and fuel consumption.

This concept takes its name from Alessandro Volta, the Italian physicist who invented the voltaic pile. Most hybrid cars are engineered for maximum economy but the Toyota Volta is an investigation into the performance potential of such a powertrain. In the Volta, the concept is so successful that maximum speed has had to be artificially capped at 155 mph (250 km/h), though the driver can still enjoy a stunning 0-62mph acceleration time of 4.0 seconds -- truly supercar performance. Despite this performance potential, thanks to a 52-litre fuel tank, the Toyota Volta also has an impressive range of at least 435 miles (700km) at highway average speeds.

The Volta is also styled like a classic supercar: it is relatively compact, with a tapered bonnet, minimum rear overhang and truncated tail. And it's also fitted with dragon-fly winged doors for maximum supercar effect.

VOLKSWAGEN W12 ROADSTER

Technical Specifications	
VW W12 Roadster	
Year	1998
Engine	5600cc W12
Power	420bhp@5,800rpm
Torque	Not quoted
0-62 mph	Not quoted
Top Speed	Not quoted
ENGINE	
Transmission	6 speed Manual
Drive	Rear-wheel drive
DIMENSIONS	
Length	4400mm
Width	1920mm

Just six months after Volkswagen W12 Syncro had been revealed at the Tokyo Show, a new roadster version was unveiled at the Geneva Show in 1998. The Syncro's four-wheel drive system was replaced by a simpler rear-wheel drive transmission, and an all-new interior was developed for the Roadster.

The W12 Roadster retained the W12 Syncro's impressive W12 engine whose four banks of three cylinders (essentially two VR6 units mated at 72 degrees) was far shorter and more compact than a conventional V12 unit. The Roadster design was more than simply the original Syncro with its roof removed. The Syncro's full-time four-wheel drive transmission was replaced by a lighter and simpler rear-wheel drive design and the Roadster also employed more standard production parts than the more conceptual Syncro had. For example, the Roadster's completely renewed interior design incorporated the instrument panel later to be fitted to a production version of the VW Polo.

With its monocoque construction, forward hinging doors in typical supercar fashion and stunning potential performance, not to mention its refined and sleek lines, this Volkswagen had truly come a long way from the original "People's Car".

VOLKSWAGEN W12 SYNCHRO

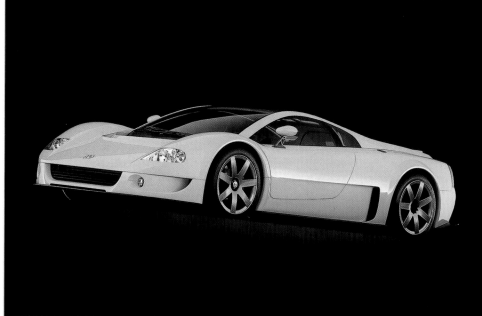

Technical Specifications

VW W12 Syncro

Year	1997
Engine	5600cc W12
Power	420bhp@5,500rpm
Torque	Not quoted
0-62 mph	Not quoted
Top Speed	Not quoted
ENGINE	
Transmission	6 speed Manual
Drive	Four-wheel drive
DIMENSIONS	
Length	4400mm
Width	1920mm

In the 1990's Audi lead the Volkswagen Group in terms of innovative concept cars but this was to change at the Tokyo Show in 1997 when VW Chairman Ferdinand Piech and Fabrizio Giugiaro of ItalDesign unveiled the W12 Syncro.

There had never been a Volkswagen like this before. VW engineers had developed an extraordinary W12 engine that was both lightweight and compact and to showcase this technology, it commissioned a running prototype from ItalDesign. Moving away from the then supercar norm, the W12 Syncro is less rounded and features sharp, even stark functional lines.

Since the purpose of this concept was to showcase VW's technology, the all-new engine is left on view beneath a large rear window and in fact even the front suspension is clearly visible beneath the massive windscreen. The engine eventually found its way into production in the Volkswagen Phaeton luxury saloon, but to date, no Volkswagen supercar has been signed off, not even one as striking as this.

Volvo 3CC

Technical Specifications	
Volvo 3CC	
Year	2005
Engine	Electric
Power	Not quoted
Torque	Not quoted
0–62 mph	10.0 sec
Top Speed	84 mph (135 km/h)
ENGINE	
Transmission	Direct drive
Drive	Front wheel drive
DIMENSIONS	
Length	3899mm
Width	1624mm

The Volvo 3CC was created at Vovlo's California studios. Its aim is to reduce both congestion and pollution, so it is small and compact and is powered by a zero-emission electric engine. This is Volvo's answer to sustainable mobility, a fuel-efficient, versatile, comfortable and safe car that's also fun to drive.

Though the 3CC is compact in its dimensions it still seats three passengers comfortably thanks to an innovative two-plus-one seating configuration which provides seating for two adults in the front and a unique rear seat solution for an additional adult or two children. The doors open upwards, and the dashboard slides forward to ease ingress and egress while a special sliding seat design assists access to the rear seats.

The Volvo 3CC has a high strength steel space frame and composite sandwich floor panels for safely and light weight. The outer body is a bonded one piece carbon fibre shell which results in a very rigid construction that provides good ride and handling. The double floor used to house the electric energy storage batteries could be adapted for virtually any other powertrain in the future, so although the 3CC is an electric vehicle, it could be powered by a petrol, diesel, biogas or even a hybrid solution.

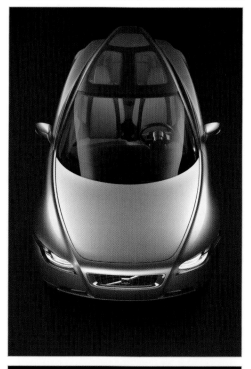

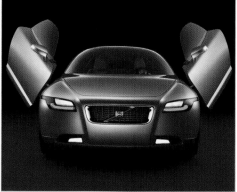

Volvo VCC

Technical Specifications	
Volvo VCC	
Year	2005
Engine	2,600cc in-line 6-cylinder
Power	250bhp
Torque	Not quoted
0-62 mph	Not quoted
Top Speed	Not quoted
ENGINE	
Transmission	6 speed Manual
Drive	Rear wheel drive
DIMENSIONS	
Length	4915mm
Width	1930mm

From the outset Volvo said this VCC concept car was more than a one-off show model – instead, it's a vision of a future Volvo V-Range car in the luxury segment. Clearly Volvo does not believe that the large luxury car is a dinosaur soon to be extinct due to its poor environmental record.

The exterior design of the VCC was a joint effort of Volvo's design studios in Barcelona in Spain and Gothenburg in Sweden. It has broad 'shoulders' and the characteristic V-shape bonnet of all Volvos. The interior reflects Scandinavian luxury with light high-quality materials and a roof panel featuring an X-frame with ambient lighting operated by slider controls in an overhead console. There are no visible air vents and air is distributed throughout the car via concealed outlets.

The VCC's engine is a 250bhp in-line six-cylinder unit with remarkably low fuel consumption thanks to new turbo technology and Direct Start & Stop, a system which automatically cuts out the engine when the car stops.

It also features Compression Auto Ignition a system in which the fuel/air mixture is compression ignited when the engine is being run gently. All this results in average fuel consumption of just 43.4mpg – highly impressive for a large luxury saloon.

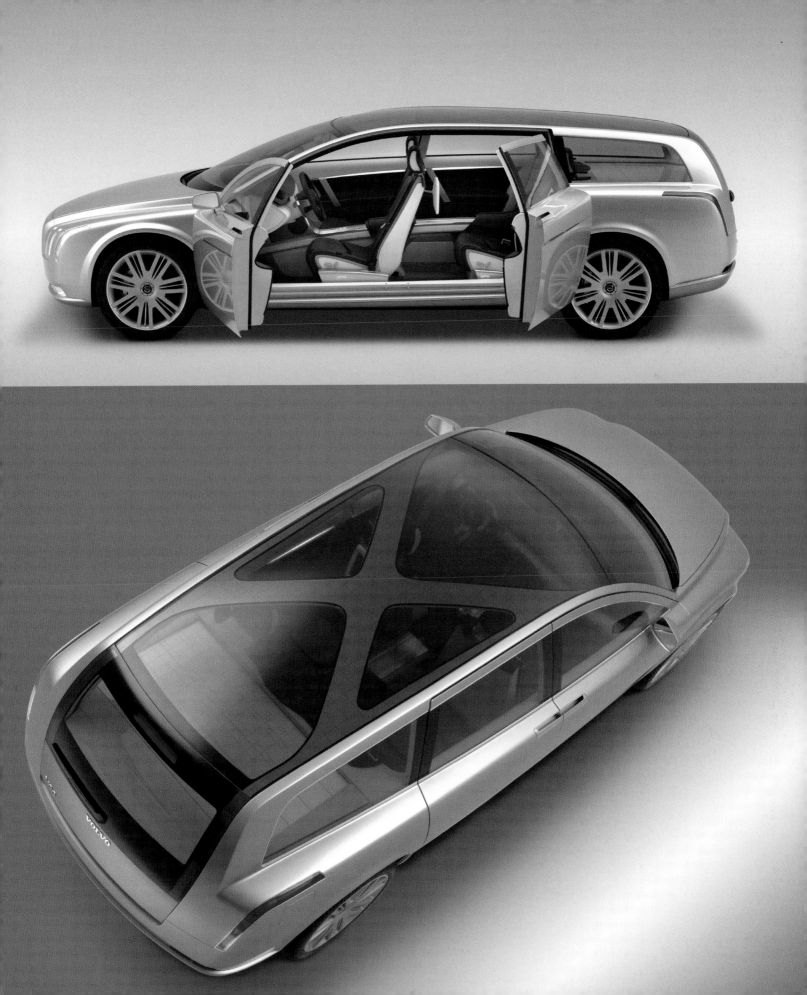

VOLVO YCC

Technical Specifications	
Volvo YCC	
Year	2005
Engine	five-cylinder PZEV
Power	215bhp
Torque	Not quoted
0-62 mph	Not quoted
Top Speed	Not quoted
ENGINE	
Transmission	6 speed Automatic
Drive	Rear wheel drive
DIMENSIONS	
Length	4400mm
Width	1830mm

The Volvo YCC is a concept car entirely devised and created by women whose brief gave them a free hand to develop a concept car capable of winning the approval of the most demanding Volvo customer of all – the independent female professional.

Volvo research shows that women buyers in the premium segment want everything that men want in terms of performance, prestige and style. But she also want more, such as smart storage, easy access and exit, good visibility, the possibility to personalize, minimal maintenance and easy parking.

Easy access is achieved via automatically opening gullwing doors; minimal maintenance results in a sealed bonnet with the driver having access only to fuel and screenwash filler caps; the seat covers can be changed so owners can personalize their car; and because bags are more often carried in the rear seats than passenger, the seats are cinema-style units that fold upwards when not in use. Storage is in a massive central console and visibility is improved thanks to narrow pillars and a personalized driving position. An autopark system measure gaps and parks the car automatically.

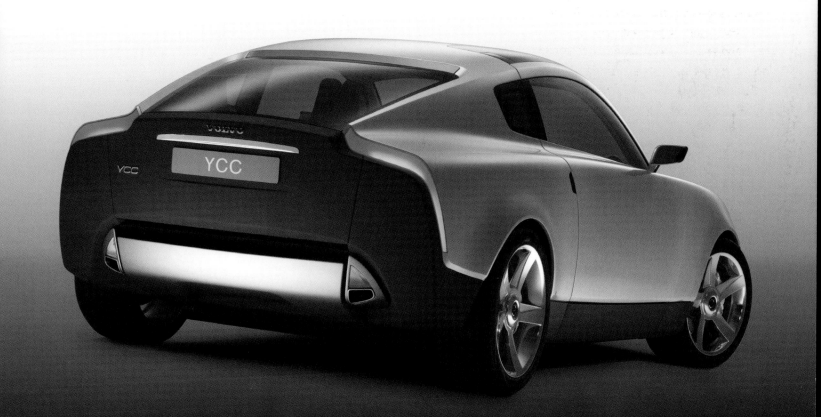

INDEX